# NARCISSISTIC RELATIONSHIP

UNDERSTANDING THE NARCISSISTIC PERSONAL-ITY DISORDER, HOW TO DEFEND YOURSELF FROM PARENTS AND PARTNER AND SAVE RELATIONSHIP.

## AUTHOR: ELLIOT FEARS

# TABLE OF CONTENTS


Introduction .................................................................1

Chapter 1 What Is A Narcissist? ...........................4

    Characteristics Of A Narcissist .........................7

    The Causes Of Narcissism ...............................11

Chapter 2 How Do Narcissistic Relationships
Happen?.....................................................................13

Chapter 3 Understanding Narcissistic Relationships...........16

Chapter 4 How Should You Deal With A Narcissist?.........22

    Acknowledgment ...............................................25

    Understanding .....................................................26

    Staying Calm......................................................27

    Relaxation ...........................................................28

    Channeling The Narcissist Out ........................29

Chapter 5 Types Of Narcissism.............................30

Chapter 6 The Phases Of A Relationship
With A Narcissist ...................................................35

    Phase 1 - The Honeymoon Phase.....................35

    Phase 2 - The Devaluation Phase .....................38

    Phase 3 - The Discard Phase ............................41

    Phase 4 - The Healing Phase............................43

Chapter 7 The Victims Of The Narcissist .............44

    Who The Narcissist Targets ..............................45

    Why The Target Stays With The Narcissist....................47

Chapter 8 Are Narcissists Victims?.......................69

Chapter 9 Escaping A Narcissistic Relationship .................73

Chapter 10 Co-Parenting With A Narcissist.......................84

Chapter 11 Recovering From A Relationship With A Narcissist.................................................................. 98

How To Avoid Being Sucked Back In ......................... 103

Learning How To Heal ................................................ 108

Chapter 12 The Steps To Healing ..................................... 113

Releasing Pain And Grieving The Relationship ........... 114

Release The Narcissistic Illusion................................. 116

Release Feelings Of Betrayal And Injustice ................. 118

Chapter 13 Tips On How To Help A Narcissist ............... 122

What Will Motivate A Narcissist To Change? ............. 123

Treatment Options ...................................................... 124

Treatment Takes Time And Effort .......................... 126

How You Can Support A Narcissist's Change.............. 127

Conclusion ....................................................................... 130

# INTRODUCTION

Everyone is classified as a narcissist at birth. Essentially, this makes sense, because right from day one out your mother's womb, you depend on everyone or someone to fulfill your every desire. Your life literally lies in someone else's care. As you grow older into a toddler and a child, you start developing a sense of personality where you push limits, test boundaries, and hold everyone else responsible for your actions because you don't know any better. You get away with things thanks to your cuteness and charm and, as long as this continues, you learn how to be narcissistic well into your adolescence. But just because we are born narcissistic does not mean we need to live with a narcissistic personality disorder.

There are three different kinds of narcissists, each with their dark traits and malicious plotting behind the scenes. Malignant narcissists, however, are sadistic by nature and also suffer from an antisocial personality disorder, which simply means they have no regard for human feelings. When we hear the term narcissist, we may stick our noses in the air or frown, because we all know what it means. If you have lived with a narcissistic spouse, then your heart may beat ten times faster for a few minutes with the overwhelming fear caused by your relationship. You may have that little voice inside your head that tells you to run, but against your better judgment, you stay because you're empathetic to their feelings. Some people don't even know they are in a narcissistic relationship because they have had their eyes blindfolded and believe the narcissist can and will change. This never comes true, though, and the abuse just continues to get worse and worse. By the end of it, you don't know what to feel – and is it the end?

Narcissists get in our heads and make us believe whatever they want us to believe, as long as they can get us to stay. We stay because we try to see the good in them, while they are only keeping us around to feed off of us and build up their narcissistic ego as a constant supply of attention. With intimacy and sprinkles of hope and love here and there, we fall even deeper into a relationship we know we shouldn't be in. The push and pull of the back and forth head games they play creates a trauma bond, which makes it even harder to leave. Do you fear your relationship? Do you fear where it's at, or where it's headed?

Have you lost more than just yourself, but your friends and, potentially, your sanity? Do you even know right from wrong anymore? When we get into relationships, we always give someone the benefit of the doubt in hopes that things won't turn out like past relationships that didn't work. When you get into a relationship with a narcissist, though, you are signing a deal with the devil without even knowing it. Before long, you become trapped, scared, miserable, and helpless as you question yourself and your reality, wondering how things became so dark.

You will learn where narcissistic personality disorder comes from, how it is developed, and how to stop it. It's never fun to be abused, but when a narcissist grabs hold of you, it can feel like your whole world comes crashing down and you don't know how to escape the darkness. You may even fear that the narcissist in you has come out and is going to unleash on all the people you care about. That is, if you haven't been completely isolated yet.

# CHAPTER 1
# WHAT IS A NARCISSIST?

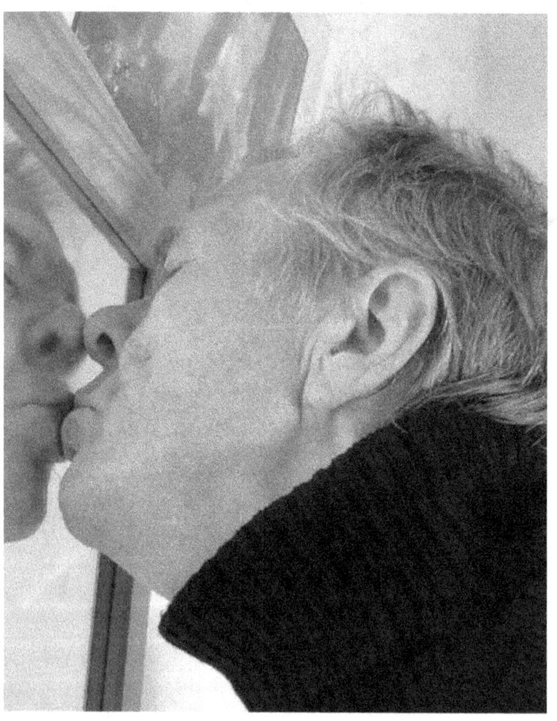

Narcissism is a personality disorder characterized by having an inflated sense of importance, a deep-seated need for excessive admiration and attention from other people and a lack of empathy for other people. This often comes off as extreme confidence but actually hides of fragile self-esteem that is vulnerable to even the slightest criticism or negative feedback. A person who is truly confident does not feel the need to brag or call attention to themselves or their achievements. This is not the case with a narcissist, who needs everyone to know about their accomplishments and about the things that make them special. This excessive bragging and boastful attitude is often a big clue in identifying a narcissist.

The narcissist feels the need to win at everything and is most often preoccupied with fantasies about the power, success, beauty, or brilliance they can amass. They need to project their fantasies. This fosters an "all about me" attitude, making the people they associate with only as valuable as how much that person can help them achieve the things they want. They do not want anyone to outshine them or else they feel the need to take that person down a notch to prove their superiority.

People who suffer from this personality disorder are generally unhappy, especially when they are not given the special treatment or admiration that they believe they deserve. This often leads to unfulfilling relationships for both themselves and others. Not only does narcissism affect the narcissist's romantic relationships in a negative way, but it can also have a poor impact on the financial affairs, school life, and work life of the narcissist.

Most people get into romantic relationships because of the need to connect with someone else and to experience feelings of love and devotion. It does not work that way with a narcissist. A narcissist is someone with extremely low self-esteem and feelings of self-worth. This person's level of self-esteem and self-worth is dependent on the admiration and attention of the other people around them. This person does not know how to love themselves, and they need other people around who are dedicated to doting on them to fill the void within themselves. That is why they enter into romantic relationships–so that someone is constantly available to stroke their ego and tend to their emotional needs. This means that they are often insensitive to the wants and needs of other people, being completely self-absorbed. This is the reason for their ability to truly connect with other people and do not feel love. They use, abuse and discard, moving on to the next target when they feel that they have used up the resources that one person has given to them.

There are two major types of narcissism. The first type is called grandiose narcissism, which is characterized by high levels of aggression, dominance, and grandiosity. People who suffer from this type of narcissism portray a higher level of outward confidence and are less sensitive to the needs and wants of other people. They were often treated as if they were superior in their early childhood and expect that treatment to continue for the rest of their lives. These types of narcissists are more likely to be unfaithful in their relationships and tend to leave more abruptly if they do not feel like a relationship caters to the special treatment that they feel that they deserve.

The other type of narcissism is called vulnerable narcissism. This type of narcissism is much more emotionally sensitive because it serves as a barrier for hiding and protecting deeper feelings of inadequacy and incompetency. Those who exhibit this type of narcissism swing back and forth between feeling superior and inferior. Instead of becoming aggressive when they feel as if they did not receive the treatment that they are entitled to, they feel victimized and anxious. This type of narcissism often develops early in childhood as a way of coping with abuse or neglect from parents or guardians. Narcissists of this kind are very possessive, paranoid, and jealous because they worry that their partner's perception of them will change.

It is good to note that narcissism is a spectrum disorder, meaning that people can display different intensities and ranges of qualities of disorder. Everyone displays some of them at some point, but it is when these behaviors become consistent over time and affect relationships that this is described as narcissism.

## Characteristics of a Narcissist

- Needing to be recognized as superior even without any achievements or accomplishments to warrant such a recognition. This is characterized by this person constantly overstating themselves because they want to be recognized as bigger and more powerful than other people.

- The exaggeration of the accomplishments, achievements and talents that this person does have. This is linked to the need to be recognized as superior. This person is not above lying about or overstating their accomplishments to gain that recognition.

- Being insistent on having the best of everything such as the best car in the parking lot. In keeping with feeling superior to other people, the narcissist needs to project that image by having the best of everything that reflects that superiority.

- Taking advantage of other people to get what he or she wants. Remember that the narcissist views other people only as valuable as they can help them, so they have no qualms about using other people to get what they want.

- The preoccupation with fantasies about having power, success, beauty, and perfection. This person has big dreams of being the biggest and best, but oftentimes, the narcissist spends more time fantasizing than putting actual work in to make these fantasies reality.

- Not taking responsibility. Since the narcissist only wants to be seen in the best light by other people, they refuse to take responsibility when something goes wrong or they are to blame for something.

- Expecting special favors and automatic compliance with the expectations of other people. The narcissist feels that his or her needs always come first and expects everyone to fall into compliance with that.

- Constantly believing that others are envious of them and, in turn, being envious of others. This occurs because the narcissist views his or herself as larger than life so, of course, others would be jealous of them. Because they are overly conscious of their image, they become quickly envious of other people who they believe are outdoing them. They often resort to name-calling, gossip, and harsh criticism to take down the person they feel is a threat to them.
- Constantly monopolizing conversations to make it about them. This ties into the narcissist feeling that everything revolves around them and their needs.
- Belittling and looking down on people that they believe are inferior to them. To keep their feeling of superiority, the narcissist feels the need to re-instate that position by belittling other people so that they are reminded of their inferiority.
- Lacking empathy. This person has an inability and willingness to recognize the needs, feelings, and wants of other people. This is what makes this person unable to love and bond with another individual.
- Being controlling and manipulative in relationships. This person expect other people to fall in line with their wants and desires so they use control and manipulation to keep the other in line

with those desires. Since they are so observant of their surroundings, they often know what strings to pull to make other people fall in line.

A narcissist often exhibits a haughty or arrogant pattern of behavior that most people consider to be boastful and pretentious. Narcissistic people feel easily slighted. Their reactions to criticism and even imagined slights range from:

- Reacting with rage and contempt and, as a result, trying to belittle the other person to make themselves feel superior.
- Having difficulty regulating their emotions and behavior and, therefore, lashing out on those around them. This can be subtle as well since the narcissist will also use underhanded tactics to get back at someone.
- Experiencing stress to change. This person likes things to be a certain way knowing that they are in control. Therefore, change is a challenge for narcissists.
- Feeling depressed or moody when they feel like they have fallen short of their expectations of perfection. Perfection is unattainable. Therefore, this is something that the narcissist constantly struggles with.
- Harboring secret feelings of insecurity, humiliation, vulnerability, and shame. At the foundation of their boastful, superior attitude, these are the

emotions the narcissist is try to hide from other people.

## The Causes of Narcissism

Narcissism is a complex personality disorder, and it is not yet known what directly causes it. However, it has been linked to the following areas:

- Genetics. Some of the characteristics that narcissistic people exhibit have been shown to be inherited. Narcissistic people often have narcissistic parents.
- Environment. Early childhood factors such as insensitive parenting, over praising and excessive pampering, excessive criticism and abuse have been shown to be common in narcissistic persons.
- Neurobiology. Studies have shown abnormalities in the genes that connects the brain to behavior.

It is good to note that narcissistic personality disorder affects men more than women and is often shown to develop in a person's teens or early childhood, even though some children show traits of narcissism.

Narcissistic people often do not recognize that they have a problem and do nothing to rectify their behavior. Many seek solace from their low self-esteem and diminished feelings of self-worth in drugs, alcohol, and other escapist habits. Even if a narcissist is aware that he or she has a problem, it may be difficult for them to seek the help and counseling that they need because reaching out may be seen as another sign of imperfection or an insult to their fragile self-esteem. However, getting the right treatment can make life more rewarding and enjoyable for not only the narcissist but those around them. A trusted doctor or mental health provider is the best person to seek help and counseling from because they can direct the narcissist in developing higher self-esteem and self-confidence, which can help balance their interactions with other people. This is especially important if the narcissist shows suicidal thoughts or behavior, suffers from anxiety and depression, or has physical health problems, all of which have been shown to be associated with narcissistic personality disorder.

To overcome narcissism, the narcissist needs to challenge his or her inner demons. Narcissists attack themselves internally and, therefore, they need to first recognize these attacks so that they can stop inflicting mental anguish on themselves and other people. It is a hard task, but the narcissist needs to differentiate his or her negative traits such as superior attitude and condescending behaviors, which results in them pushing other people away and sabotaging they're entire life.

Only then they can break the cycle of seeking emotional sustenance from other people in such a destructive way. The narcissist needs to foster self-compassion so that they can evaluate themselves in a way that is kind and mindful. It is possible to come back from narcissism.

# CHAPTER 2
# HOW DO NARCISSISTIC
# RELATIONSHIPS HAPPEN?

Even the best of us fall for people that we shouldn't. Sometimes we ignore the signs and our intuition warning us that these people are bad for us because they appeal to us so greatly.

Sometimes, though, a toxic relationship occurs not because we ignore the signs that we should steer clear. It occurs because the signs were not there at the beginning. These types of relationships occur because the person we entered that relationship with was good at disguising their true selves from us. This is the case when most narcissistic relationships occur–the other person gets swept in the facade that the narcissist projects and, by the time they catch on to the deceit, they are caught in the narcissist's web of lies.

Don't feel ashamed that you fell for a narcissist or even that you felt desperate to hang on to the union that you two have or had. A narcissist is a smart person and a liar. This person is very skilled at hiding the negative qualities of his or her character when you first meet them. This person is charismatic and careful to keep the other person under their charming spell. Narcissists are often widely labeled as chameleons because they are so good at adapting their behavior to the situations and persons that they encounter. Just like the animal, they are skilled at changing their colors to adapt to the environment that they are in.

When approaching a romantic relationship, a narcissist is generous, attentive, kind and seemingly selfless. This person is charming and quick to give compliments. Narcissists often approach a new relationship with an intensity that sweeps the other person off their feet and makes them feel as if they are the most beautiful and talented person on the planet. Narcissists make promises that go to the heart of what the other person wants. They make the other person come alive with emotion and inject confidence in the relationship that is mesmerizing. It is this mesmerizing that makes the other party blind to the unpleasant qualities they may have let slip through the cracks.

However, slowly but surely, the narcissist's true nature comes out and the relationship starts to come apart at the seams. By the time the red flags are showing, we are often too deeply involved with this person to simply end the relationship. We are still too wrapped in the grand possibilities for the future that's injected into our minds and hearts. To understand how a narcissist hooks someone else into believing that a relationship with them will work and then keeping the other person hooked even after their negative qualities show, we need to take a look at the phases of how a narcissistic relationship starts and ends. Each phase has specific qualities that show just how difficult it is to be free of this person even when not in a union with them.

After being in a relationship with a narcissist and going through these phases, it will feel like you had been on a rollercoaster ride where the highs were extremely high and the lows were just as extreme. These phases engage the emotions of the victimized party, hence why they remain in the relationship longer than they should, while the narcissist remains disengaged and calculating how their can benefit from the situation.

Before we move on to these phases and why they work the way that they do, let's take a moment to look into the mind of a narcissist. This analyzation will help you understand this rollercoaster ride of extreme ups and downs.

# CHAPTER 3
# UNDERSTANDING NARCISSISTIC RELATIONSHIPS

Should I stay or should I go? That's the question most people ask themselves when they find themselves tied to an abusive or narcissistic spouse. Most times, it is people who are empathetic or codependent who attract narcissists. People who are selfish, egocentric, cynical, disagreeable, and mentally or emotionally abusive are those who have narcissistic traits. However, narcissism is present in every person of the human race – it's only when someone obtains these traits and employs them across all aspects of their life that they suffer with narcissistic personality disorder (NPD). People with narcissistic personality disorder often don't realize they are narcissists because of the way they were raised, usually by a narcissistic parent. For them, emotional unavailability, criticism, high expectations, and sense of entitlement is normal. Although there is no reason for someone to blame, victimize, control, and manipulate, a narcissist does these things out of low self-esteem and low self-confidence.

So, what is narcissistic personality disorder? Narcissism can be healthy, even essential for a well-balanced personality. Healthy narcissism is when someone is selfish in their own growth, but not self-centered to the point where they use others to gain personal growth. It's when someone likes attention, but also knows how to give attention to someone else. In general, healthy narcissism is when someone is selfish enough to go after their dreams and strive for success, but also have the empathy to build and maintain strong relationships. In a sense, someone who has high levels of emotional intelligence can be defined as developing healthy narcissism.

On the other hand, someone diagnosed with narcissistic personality disorder is someone who lacks empathy for others, where they don't care about someone else's thoughts and feelings. NPD is when someone experiences a fantasized exaggerated grandiose image of themselves and craves attention and admiration, among many other characteristics such as:

- Has the opposite of emotional intelligence
- Has an excessive need for recognition and praise
- Believes they are superior to everyone else (usually fantasized)
- Seeks money, power, control, etc. with manipulation tactics
- Lacks empathy
- Uses people to get what they want without considering the consequences
- Usually has an arrogant or cocky persona

Narcissistic personality disorder is not genetic, although it appears to look that way as it can be passed down through generations. Every child is influenced by their parent or caregiver, so if the parent suffers with NPD, their children will most likely turn out narcissistic as well. Narcissistic parents expect too much of their children and, since they lack empathy, they often disregard their child's needs, wants, and desires – especially when the child develops a sense of independence. In a narcissist's eyes, their child is on this Earth to serve them.

Essentially, they see their children as an extension of themselves.

The parent will become envious, cynical, and even competitive when it comes to their children's success. Narcissists feel entitled to everything, so when their child succeeds, they steal the spotlight and make their children feel unappreciated, which promotes codependent behavior into adulthood. As the child grows, they learn that they get love and attention only if they gain the approval of their caregiver. As a result, the child will always try to improve, impress, and strive for perfection as they continuously seek validation. Validation-seekers often become people-pleasers, attention-searchers, and manipulators, as this behavior is what has seemed to work for them throughout their lives. Into adulthood, when someone gets intimately involved with a partner, they will use behaviors such as manipulation, control, people-pleasing, and lying to obtain love and acceptance from their spouse.

In the beginning of any relationship, there is a honeymoon stage where the couple is new, fresh, and has a lust for each other. A narcissist can be extremely charming, because they give their 'victim' or potential partner attention and affection as long as they are receiving it in return. Gradually, as the relationship progresses, the narcissist will give less and less attention to their spouse, because they have gotten comfortable with the effort and affection their partner gives to them. Their partner, on the other hand, may suffer feelings of loneliness and betrayal, and longs for their lover's affection. With one of the characteristics of a narcissist being lack of empathy, they will rarely notice their spouse's feelings and when brought up, the narcissist will disregard their spouse's feelings in an attempt to shy away from the guilt or blame that they are even doing anything wrong.

Malignant narcissists, however, do not feel as though they ever do anything wrong and will continue to devalue their partner on purpose. A malignant narcissist is the most dangerous narcissist of them all.

In a narcissistic relationship, you may feel as though your boundaries and privacy are not being respected. As much as your narcissistic partner says that they understand or that they will try harder, or maybe even apologizes, they only continue to repeat their patterns. This is mainly because they did not receive the proper guidance growing up – their boundaries were disrespected, which left them feeling abandoned and unloved, or rather, loved conditionally. The effect this has on the spouse is that they may be fearful to express themselves emotionally or set boundaries. The thing about narcissistic relationships is that narcissists will sprinkle some light into your day in an attempt to keep you around. Someone suffering from this abuse will often ask themselves if they did this one more thing, would something change. An empathic person is willing to give their partner the 'benefit of the doubt' countless times, in an effort to fix their spouse or help their partner. However, a narcissist will never change unless they see there is a problem. Although this does happen, it is very rare for a narcissist to see that anything – especially their own behavior – is wrong.

Narcissists have deep-rooted and deep-bred low self-esteem issues based on their upbringing. With that said, they usually grow up bullying others to get their way and, as they grow into adolescence, they start to figure out how manipulation works. At home, they see their parents getting away with controlling their environment, using people to get their way, and holding a high self-image on the exterior, and this type of behavior is something they will try. Due to the lack of empathy caused by the lack of attention and guidance they saw growing up, they are taught that emotions are not needed and will often hide or repress their own feelings. When someone else shows vulnerability by being upset or angry, the narcissist ignores their emotions and often, they don't realize they have hurt or caused emotional pain to their partners. The abuse that comes from a narcissist can include:

- Emotional abandonment

- Neglect
- Manipulation
- Brainwashing
- Gaslighting
- Ignoring their partners
- Crossing boundaries
- Invading space and privacy
- Blaming
- Guilting

Among other shameful abusive tactics, narcissists don't see their wrong-doing because when they abuse, they are only acting upon what they were taught and influenced by. A covert narcissist will often act passive-aggressively towards their spouse, then justify their actions through lies or gaslighting. Unless a narcissist has experienced an all-time blow to their image or ego, they will not seek guidance or therapy to 'change,' as they are happy getting what they want through their abusive behavior. They also don't see anything wrong, so counseling for their personality is foreign to them.

# CHAPTER 4
# HOW SHOULD YOU DEAL WITH A NARCISSIST?

With narcissists, it is very easy for us to shift our focus onto them, mainly because we often we feel like we have no choice and as if we are being forced into those frustrating interactions with them. There is no way of navigating our own feelings and emotions when a narcissist is around because they are so vindictive and demanding of our undivided attention that it becomes increasingly more difficult for us to function at a normal, clear-minded level. We find this mentally destabilizing and the hardest part about interactions with a narcissist is the normalization period after where we sit in utter bewilderment, struggling to comprehend how such a person can take such a mental toll on our minds.

Narcissism - or rather people who have Narcissistic Personality Disorder – is not just a personality disorder. It is an array of traits and characteristics in which congregate and formulate within someone's identity. A narcissist's identity is an infliction in itself. They have a heightened sense of identity, meaning that they are individuals who only see the best in themselves, although exaggeratedly, and cannot see their own faults and flaws. Like with Narcissus, his successors only see their best reflection, one that only reflects positivity, beauty, and success, and this develops, in their minds at least, that they deserve recognition from us for all of that. They embody an unnatural yet common persona of "gods amongst men". And this, though buried deep within a narcissist is a sensitive being, affects us – people who are not narcissists – even more. A narcissist's words and way of exuberant bragging degrade us and that degradation is unhealthy for us. It breeds self-doubt, it impairs our ability to succeed because we believe the judgment of someone who themselves cannot stand – or even believe – judgment. They are critical of us and we need to learn how to deal with them.

Let us go back to that word. Sensitive. Narcissists are sensitive individuals who lack empathy and outward emotion towards others, yet possess such a deep and in-tune emotional connection with themselves. This makes them highly oblivious to their own faults and flaws which, in turn, when pointed out to them, they simply cannot believe you. So creates a grudge which can often linger for months to years to a lifetime. Narcissists are, staying with sensitivity, incredibly reactive to rejection. This could be towards how they look, what they do for a living, what they have said, and their opinion. Remember, a narcissist is "always right" and for you to challenge that stance often has a more hurtful outcome for you. Why? Because we cannot win against or challenge a narcissist and that is something we must deal with.

However, with this said, do not make promises with a narcissist. To rephrase that – do not allow yourself to believe that a promise made by a narcissist will be seen through and kept. Though a narcissist will never forget a grudge or a person who "once said something about me", they will almost always "forget" a promise made. A reason for this could be that we have already given the narcissist what they want and they have simply moved on. The best piece of advice for this, if a narcissist has made a promise with you, is to be persistent in order to make sure that their word is kept. Yes, in a way, this is challenging the narcissist, though this route is not challenging their credibility.

Dealing with narcissists is something we have all done and gone through and through those interactions we know now that dealing with narcissists is like dealing with a hostage situation; something can always go wrong and we will feel the effects of that for a very long, long time. Narcissists have this austere and gravitas about them that sometimes, when dealing with relationships, can come across as them being charismatic, which at first is true. However, this is an effect of them being the one in control of every possible outlet and outcome of the relationship through their campaign of strong manipulation. How can we tell when they are manipulating us? Assess the situation as a politician would when dealing with a conflict resolution crisis in some foreign country- look at the situation, how it has benefited you, the narcissist, and then see who it really has benefitted. The answer will often shock you.

With a narcissist, think of them as the driver of the fancy car with you next to them in some dingy wagon, even if you both drive the same car – such is the gravitational pull to their perfect selves and lives that they will idealize themselves, congratulate themselves, shower themselves with praise and adulation, and try to outdo whatever it is that you have ever accomplished. The point being: we will always be a backseat passenger when it comes to our friendships, relationships, and associations with a narcissist, never at the wheel or beside them.

We need to accept that there simply is no win-win outcome with a narcissist.

But how can we deal with them? There are three main ways of dealing with a narcissist – acknowledgment and understanding. There are other methods that we could use that would be beneficial to us when dealing with a narcissist, such as staying calm, relaxation, channeling the narcissist out, or deeper psychological methods (when in a toxic relationship with one) such as therapy and meditation.

## Acknowledgment

When we are dealing with a narcissist whose opinion seems to be the only one that "should be taken into account" we can simply acknowledge the narcissist, thank them for their opinion, and then to make sure that we have made certain that they seem sure that we appreciate their opinion. We can thank them and do whatever we want with that information. By acknowledging the narcissist's opinion we have navigated a safer route around the definite feeling of scorn that would have otherwise been directed towards us by the narcissist. By doing this we have been the "adult" in the situation and have seemingly heightened the narcissist's self-esteem by making them think that we will use their advice and suggestions, even though to a degree we will not be taking it into consideration. Avoiding the conflict which comes from challenging the narcissist's opinion allows us to show an interest in what the narcissist has said.

## Understanding

Though acknowledging a narcissist implies that we listen and do not take into consideration, understanding the narcissist is by actually listening to them and taking into account what they have said is a little bit more complex. Though this tactic can usually save us from the wrath of the narcissist, understanding their opinion takes a little more nous. We need to make sure that we let them know that we value them and then listen to what they have said, keenly listening until, from underneath all that self-absorbed theory, we can piece together our own picture of what they have said. This can be entirely frustrating but it is something that sometimes we should do. Behind their mask is someone who has gotten to the top quickly, despite stepping on everyone to get there. Often, when we dissect what they have said and omitted the spotlight fever connotations we can actually get a clear picture of what they are talking about, thus meaning that the advice they have given can actually be applied to a certain situation in which we are going through. For instance, someone with NPD explains their success in such detail, as they usually do, we hear bits and pieces of information which makes us think, "Hang on a minute. That is actually quite sound advice" Yes, the underlying argument is how they are so successful or how they did some amazing thing over the weekend, but somewhere in that mix is something useful. Understanding the narcissist is a heat-deflector and grudge-deflator.

## Staying Calm

If you are not a person who can easily deal with a narcissist then staying calm is by far the most difficult practice for you when they start going on about this and that. It irks you, creates this massive bubble of steaming water that wants to spill over. We all have been there, don't worry. It is that feeling when what they have said is so mean or just dumbfounded that we ball up our fists, sigh, smile, and nod our heads; that frustration that is about to explode; the emotion of complete and utter anger that fills us and consumes us. But we can deal with that emotion. It takes time to perfect it but staying calm, especially when the narcissist you are around is persistent in his or her presentation of themselves, can be a life-changing tool in being at peace with the situation or interaction. Sure, it is extremely difficult but acceptance of that situation or interaction with the narcissist and then finding a small piece of calm within you can certainly go a long way. For instance, a narcissist starts explaining all that you did wrong, whether this narcissist is someone at work or your loved one, and you become awash with anger but know how the narcissist will react, do you shout and go off and get nowhere with the narcissist or do you try your best to stay calm, listen, and then just move on? Everybody snaps eventually and that is our human nature, our survival instincts kicking in. It is a normal reaction. It is the pressure building up and our tempers becoming unhinged. But, we do need to be aware that by arguing with or retorting back at a narcissist only affects you and not them.

## Relaxation

Relaxation is an important part of everyone's lives, including the narcissist. But for us who are dating or married to a narcissist, friends with one, or the narcissist happens to be your mother or father, finding time to get away from the hounding madness that usually ensues when in their company is a valuable asset in managing your emotional and mental strength. Constantly listening can switch you off, make you feel unmotivated, and hurt you. It can drive you mad and can drive you away in tears. But finding somewhere where you can essentially switch off and switch back on again is paramount. Hiking, running, a beach walk. Clarity is the best natural and mental healer. It allows for storage space to be freed up and offers you the platform to think. There are so many forms of relaxation that can really refresh someone. Renew yourself away from the narcissistic atmosphere and remove yourself from the narcissistic environment in which you live or work in. Even if this is for ten minutes, finding that balance again is important when dealing with a narcissist.

## Channeling the Narcissist Out

This is the opposite of acknowledging and understanding a narcissist. channeling out the narcissist is the basic term for I do not want to be around you because you make me feel worthless for your own personal gain. Another way of saying this could be that you have taken the decision to cut out the narcissist in your life who has had a negative impact on you mentally and physically. Although, yes, the attachment to them is quite strong and the process will be difficult, the step forward for you will have such positive effects on your life. However, channeling out a narcissist can also be someone at work who you have chosen not to listen to because of their self-centered nature. This could have a big impact on your work life, whereas before you had to deal with the feeling of doubt and hurt, you can now flourish in an environment where you are more comfortable, at peace, and at ease without the mental strain of being around the narcissist.

# CHAPTER 5
# TYPES OF NARCISSISM

There are three types of narcissists: the classical, the covert, and the malignant, which range from mild to extreme (extreme being the malignant narcissist). A malignant narcissist is the most destructive, self-involved, hostile, and abusive. Furthermore, a covert narcissist – also known as the vulnerable narcissist – is more discreet in their ways, but it doesn't mean they are any less dangerous. For example, someone can live with and even marry a covert narcissist without ever knowing that they are in love with one. A classic narcissist is the one most people think about when they think of narcissism. NPD sufferers are generally described as having a sense of entitlement due to their grandiose fantasies of themselves, while using manipulation tactics to gain personal success and power over others. Due to the narcissist's low self-esteem, they are very sensitive to criticism, so lashing out with malicious behavior is the result of their repressed anger to protect their fragile egos.

Each of the three types of narcissists have subtypes and do not all act the same way, as every narcissist has their own way of thinking and perceiving. The one thing they do have in common is their fragile egos with their inse-curities resulting from childhood experiences.

Classic Narcissists:

Classic narcissists are the ones that people think of when they hear the word 'narcissist.' This type of narcissist sets the definition of narcissism for the other two types. They get bored easily while stealing the spotlight or 'taking up all the air' in the room when they aren't interested in a conversation. They expect high praise as they crave an excessive amount of attention, while at the same time have the belief that they are better than others.

You will often find classic narcissists bragging about their achievements or exaggerating their stories as a way to compete or 'one-up' someone else.

Vulnerable Narcissists:

Also known as a fragile or covert narcissist, these narcissists avoid the spotlight but still feel superior and expect individual attention. Rather than finding attention or stealing the show from someone, they will attach themselves to another individual and use them to treat themselves. The reason these types of narcissists often go unnoticed is because they will play the 'poor me' card and guilt others as a way to get admiration. In other words, vulnerable narcissists can be quite vindictive, manipulative, and discreet in their abuse.

Malignant Narcissists:

This type of narcissist is the most dangerous, also known as toxic, and are highly manipulative and exploitative as one of their main traits is sadism. Their narcissistic personality disorder is often also accompanied by antisocial personality disorder, which is why malignant narcissists are so dangerous. Alongside their lack of empathy for others and their sadistic nature, their dissocial personality makes them impulsive and aggressive in their behavior. This antisocial disorder is not prominent in the other two types of narcissism, and is often the main characteristic of a psychopath or sociopath. The malignant narcissist disregards all feelings, has low morals, doesn't care about consequences and will go out of their way to dominate and control people around them. It is said that malignant narcissists have no remorse for their behavior and may actually enjoy torturing others.

Subtype one – Overt vs. Covert

Overt refers to the way a malignant narcissist would do things – manipulation, brainwashing, and disregarding feelings openly.

Covert is more the way a vulnerable narcissist would operate – making people pity them, guilting someone, and looking for opportunities to manipulate someone in a more secretive measure. Both overt and covert subtypes are prideful and abusive, however overt narcissists abuse in a way that is noticeable and uncaring. Covert s take more time to plot, plan, and when they see an opportunity, they will undeniably strike.

These covert types abuse gradually and keep the 'spark' of the relationship going for quite some time before they show their other side. A malignant narcissist can be covert or overt in their abusive ways, whereas an overt is always the classic and a covert is always the vulnerable narcissist.

Subtype two – Somatic vs. Cerebral These subtypes are defined by the narcissist's core values in themselves. Narcissists can never be outshined by their significant other – or anyone, for that matter. Their view on their partners and even their children is that they are a prize to show off to the rest of the world. Somatic narcissists are fixated and completely concerned with their own image. You will find these narcissists at the gym, going for jogs, eating a healthy diet, and maintaining an attractive body. Cerebral narcissists are the brains of the operation. These narcissists are smart and show off their intellect by boasting or competing about their smarts when in conversations. They often impress people with their accomplishments and are usually found to be the 'head guy' in most companies. However, not every top leader is a narcissist, and not every fit person is narcissistic. All three narcissists can be somatic and cerebral narcissists.

Subtype three – Inverted

An inverted narcissist is the type who victimizes their predators.

In other words, an inverted narcissist is the narcissist who gets in relationships with other narcissists. They are seen as codependent and attach themselves to other narcissists to gain admiration and acceptance. A covert or vulnerable narcissist can be the inverted subtype, and usually suffer from a neglectful childhood.

As much as it is beneficial for you to research about narcissism and the various types, it is crucial for your mental, physical, and emotional health to rid yourself of toxic people altogether.

# CHAPTER 6
# THE PHASES OF A RELATIONSHIP WITH A NARCISSIST

A narcissistic relationship often follows a general pattern that is easily distinguished if you know the signs to look for. This three-phase cycle can repeat several times if the victim is accepting of the narcissist coming back into their life time and time again, which happens if the narcissist needs to feed off the emotional energy that they can gain from the victim.

## Phase 1 - The Honeymoon Phase

This stage can go by many names in addition to the honeymoon phase. These include the love phase and the overvaluation phase. This is because there is an excess of "positive" feelings here with lots of grand professions of love and commitment. This occurs because the narcissist places the other person on a pedestal and makes them feel worshipped. The aim is to make that other person fall in love with them. The narcissist chooses this person carefully, targeting them for some reason such as their social status, looks, popularity, or wealth. The more that the narcissist feels that he or she can gain from this person, the higher the value he or she places on roping that person into becoming their partner. The narcissist gets tunnel vision and becomes relentless in the pursuit of that person. They devote time and energy into showering that person with compliments and attention. To the other person, it will feel like they are being swept off their feet.

The narcissist benefits from this phase because they will feel loved and idolized by that person as well. Their self-esteem and self-worth is boosted by the hopes and dreams the other person places on this relationship. The other person is thinking about them constantly and there is nothing a narcissist loves more than being the center of someone else's attention. At this point the narcissist is infatuated.

The person who didn't see this feels as if they have found a soulmate because the narcissist will have devoted time and attention into learning the ins-and-outs of what pleases them and gives the illusion that they can provide it. They feel as if they found the one–the person who is in tune with their beliefs, dreams, and aspirations for the future–and let down their guard because they feel accepted by the narcissist.

This is the stage where the other person develops a dependency on the narcissist. Because of the extreme emotions that the narcissist invoked from other people, they have created a dependency and need for validation from them. The other party may have never needed this validation from another person before, but that can easily change when in a relationship with a narcissist. This is because the narcissist gives this validation freely and frequently at this phase of the relationship. You will feel a reward, and the brain gets hooked on the gratification is receives when the narcissist dishes out that reward. There is science behind this.

There is an internal infrastructure network in the brain called the reward system. This system is activated by rewarding or reinforcing external stimulation like positive words and even drugs like heroin. When this system is activated, the brain releases feel-good hormones such as dopamine, which makes the person feel good. This system affects learning, decision-making, and elicits positive emotions such as pleasure. The mind has a constant craving for the things that activate this reward system and will associate closely with these things, such as affirmations from a narcissist. It will crave activation as often as possible and seeks the things that causes it.

This is how deeply a narcissist sinks their claws into another person at this phase of a relationship. They literally make the other person addicted to them…

Do not despair or think that you can never let your guard down with another romantic interest. The trick to steering clear of this danger in the early part of a relationship, whether it is with a narcissist or not, is to never give too much of yourself upfront. While it is, of course, essential that you let your walls down enough build a connection with another human being in a romantic sense, you always need to prioritize protecting your emotions and your mental health first.

## Phase 2 - The Devaluation Phase

In this phase, the narcissist begins to reveal his or her true colors, now feeling secure and confident that they have secured the love and devotion of the target. They will become distant and pull away from the other person. This can happen in gradual increments or seemingly overnight.

The attention and compliments will turn into indifference and silence. It is not uncommon for a narcissist to suddenly go weeks without allowing contact between themselves and the person that they pursued so relentlessly in phase 1. This leaves the other person feeling confused and wondering what they did wrong. In fact, more than likely, no matter what the narcissist does, the victim will still feel like they have the ultimate love for this person and that they cannot survive without them. This is called "Stockholm Syndrome," which was coined after a robbery in Stockholm in 1973, where the hostages of that robbery developed positive feelings toward the robbers even though they were targeted by the captives.

At this stage in the relationship, the narcissist is likely bored because the high of the pursuit in the beginning of the relationship is gone. The void that they were trying to fill with the other person's love and devotion is apparent to them once more, and they begin to question their self-worth.

This imbalance makes the narcissist moody and easily agitated, and it is at this time they will blame the other party for anything that goes wrong, and withdraw increasingly from that person. At this point, the other person, who has gotten used to the time, attention, and compliments that the narcissist used to give during the love phase of this relationship, tries to cling to what used to be. This has the opposite effect that this person wants because the harder they cling to a narcissist, the more the narcissist withdraws from them, often increasing that person's emotional torment with blame and criticism. The narcissist will cut down this person's confidence and erode their self-esteem with barbs such as criticisms on their personal appearance and other types of insults. The narcissist will use that person as their emotional, verbal, and sometimes physical punching bag. The narcissist is also a pathological liar and when confronted about the lying, cheating and dishonest behavior, they will turn it around so that the other person is left feeling like they did something wrong. This stage of a relationship with a narcissist is characterized by a lot of anger and fighting.

The reason most people do not leave a relationship at this point is because they are desperately trying to find what they fell in love with at the beginning of the relationship, not realizing that this person never existed. They unknowingly fell for an illusion. They fall into an emotional turmoil, unfortunately mirroring what goes on inside the mind and heart of a narcissist.

The solution to surviving this part of a relationship with a narcissist is to engage your other interests, which you should never give up. The narcissist will attempt to isolate you and take you away from your hobbies, friends, family and other interests during the first phase of the relationship. They will try to make your world revolve around them. Do not let this happen. This treatment is wrong and harmful to your mental and emotional health. Always ensure that you have other interests in your life that you can fall back on, especially when you are going through a hard time.

In addition, if you are at this stage, you need to realize that you need to let people go if they have grown distant. Do not chase after someone who does not want to be caught. You need to gather up the pieces of your self-esteem and realize that someone who truly loves you will not put you through that type of turmoil.

Also, fighting and approaching situations with anger rarely solves the problem. Confrontation certainly never works with a narcissist because they usually counter with the silent treatment, which forces the other person to feel like they are the party in the wrong. This often leaves the other person feeling the need to apologize. The solution here is to remove yourself from the encounter. Do not use anger, and do not be roped in by the silent treatment.

This phase is also characterized by a lot of self-blame on the victim's part, which is just part of the narcissists manipulative ploy. They use words and silence to make the victim feel at fault. This process of making someone else feel like they did something wrong when they didn't is called gaslighting. If you feel you are to blame for the things going wrong in your relationship, objectively examine the things that have been said and done. If you are in or were in a relationship with a narcissist, you will realize that this breakdown in the union is not to be placed solely on your shoulders.

## Phase 3 - The Discard Phase

After a narcissist has taken all that he or she requires out of a relationship such as the inflation of his or her ego, the flattery of being seen with a popular figure or even money, this person will simply walk away from the relationship with an ease that will show that their feelings were never engaged in the first place. This is often done cruelly and abruptly, leaving the victim who had been in this relationship with a narcissist to try to put the pieces back together. The victim is often left a shadow of their former selves and has to put in a lot of work to rebuild best self-esteem and self-confidence.

Even more cruel than simply ending the relationship, the narcissist will sometimes drag the victim along with the false hope that things will work out. Most of the time, the victim goes along with this because the narcissist has thoroughly convinced them that no one else will love them. This is just one of the many manipulative tactics the narcissist uses to keep the victim in his or her life to use as they see fit. This is a lie, of course.

If you find yourself at this phase of a narcissistic relationship, try your hardest to walk away when you see no real effort on the part of the narcissist to mend the relationship. A lot of people try to hold onto this relationship because they believe that the narcissist will change, but that is an unlikely prospect because most narcissists do not see the fault in themselves. This person is void of empathy and deep feelings directed toward anyone other than themselves. There is nothing you or anyone else can do to fix that.

You need to block all contact with the narcissist because even though they have discarded the victim, there is always the possibility that they will pop back up in the person's life no matter how much time has passed. The narcissist still sees the value in what the victim provided and reserves the right to go back for more at any time. If the victim allows it, then the cycle will start back up with a watered down version of phase 1. The victim needs to be able to stand their ground and not allow this cycle to keep on repeating itself.

It can also help to seek the counsel of a therapist to help you make it through this stage. This licensed professional can give you great insight into the relationship you had and also help you rebuild your self-esteem.

## Phase 4 - The Healing Phase

This stage is not a part of being in a relationship with a narcissist but about the recovery and healing of the victim after. This phase involves accepting that the narcissist you had been in a relationship with is a damaged person, and no amount of help and support from you can fix this person. The victim needs to realize that they need to direct the healing energy inward so that they can put the shattered pieces of their heart and mind back together. Be strong, know that this is not your fault and know that you can be better. All you need to do is take it one day at a time.

The thing to concentrate on is that you are now free of this person's control and manipulation. You can now focus totally in improving your life, which should now be a lot calmer and less stressful now that this person is out of the picture. It is time to make yourself your highest priority so that you do not fall into the same trap ever again.

# CHAPTER 7
# THE VICTIMS OF THE NARCISSIST

Everyone who interacts with the narcissist is a potential victim. As the narcissist perceives all around them as less than themselves and places little store on the safety and security of others, the harm that such a person does to its victims can be wanton and extreme. As has been previously stated, the victims of the narcissist are sometimes unaware that they are victims, which makes them perfect prey for a predator that lacks empathy for others.

Although the victim of the narcissist is typically the person closest to them, the narcissist has the potential to abuse or destroy anyone emotionally. Many people who read about narcissism are the significant other or child of a narcissist, but education on this condition is also valuable to someone sharing an office or a flat with such people.

Some may be reticent to see themselves as "victims." It has been argued by some social scientists and others that we live in a culture of victimhood and that it is dysfunctional and entitled to men and women to perceive themselves as such. That being said, it is obvious to anyone who studies narcissism that the narcissist victimizes people, whether we want to label such people victims or not. The narcissist has been known to destroy the lives of others, leading to isolation from the outside world, complete mental breakdown, or death in such cases. You may decide that you would rather not think of yourself as a victim (if you have been targeted by the narcissist), and you are perfectly within your rights to do so. However, the actions of the narcissist are those of a person who lacks empathy and is, therefore, inclined to make others into victims of their whims.

## Who the Narcissist Targets

The narcissist sees all people as fodder for their manipulation and abuse because they see others as extensions of their will. In short, the narcissist does not perceive the selves as others as being the same as their own self, if they recognize the selves of others at all. This is a concept that is important to understand in narcissism as it underlies much of their victimization.

This does not mean that the narcissist does not feel emotion. They do, but they frequently hide their emotions because they recognize how emotion can be used. When a narcissist does display emotion, it is often rage resulting from the anger they feel when they do not get what they want. Because the narcissist uses emotion as a tool, they tend to target people who are more sensitive to emotion and suggestible emotionally.

The empath is a typical target of the narcissist because of their emotional awareness and sensitivity. The empath is someone who naturally forms emotional connections with others, which enables them to rather quickly and effortlessly experience the subjective emotions of others. The narcissist is able to use the empath's sensitivity against them in several spheres, but two, in particular, stand out. The narcissist will use the empath's sensitivity to establish an emotional rapport with the empath as a first step towards manipulation and mind control. The narcissist will also use the empath's sensitivity to hurt them as part of establishing a subservient relationship dynamic and to keep them in the relationship.

The narcissist targets empaths and other emotionally sensitive people because it is easier for the narcissist to control them than other people. Someone who is not particularly sensitive, aloof, or not especially interested in closeness with others will be harder for the narcissist to establish rapport with and control as they will be somewhat immune to the typical tactics that the narcissist uses.

## Why the Target Stays with the Narcissist

When one thinks about how the narcissist gains influence over their target, it is not difficult to understand why the target remains in the relationship, even to their own detriment. The target is an emotionally aware person who enjoys closeness with others and naturally establishes emotional bonds. The target will have established a bond with the narcissist. This is because of the strategies the narcissist has engaged in to accomplish this.

In other words, the target will remain in a relationship with the narcissist because they have become close to the narcissist. They may see the narcissist as a loving and good person who generally cares about them when this is, in fact, not who the narcissist is at all. It can be important for the narcissist to do some reality testing in order to get an accurate sense of who the narcissist is. Was the narcissist there for you when you really needed someone? Does the narcissist make you feel better or worse? Do you have a mental list of all of the bad things that the narcissist had done to you? Approaching matters this way can help you realize that the narcissist is not the loved one you perhaps thought they were, but someone who is not actually capable of loving you.

Narcissism as Related to our Life

Only about one percent of the population has been diagnosed with narcissistic personality disorder (NPD), however many people do possess similar traits to that of a narcissist. The word narcissist is even becoming more common, used in daily dialogue. Although one percent seems low bear in mind almost every narcissist sees nothing wrong in their lives and do not seek any treatment.

Usually, when a narcissist has been diagnosed or is seeking some form of treatment it is usually because a significant other or person who loves them can no longer suffer the wrath of being in a narcissistic relationship. This relationship is not always in the form of significant others; it could be your parent or guardian, even your boss.

An emotionally immature person will go searching for validation of their worth, have low self-esteem, and feel inferior. Being emotionally immature can lead to a series of neurosis including paranoia and narcissism. Many psychologists believe that this neurosis can lead people to become insecure, vacillating, and obedient. Once these traits start taking over to counter that empty void feeling they are left with often the narcissist will now start creating situations where they are the center of attention.

Another response to feeling substandard or inferior is to create a superiority complex. By creating this false bravado around themselves, the narcissist will believe they are better than anyone therefore not having to listen to what other people have to say and to belittle. Belittling them is another approach many bullies use to make sure people will fear them because if they fear the narcissist his façade will never be questioned. Paranoia and envy are characteristics always found in the narcissist.

There is a difference in narcissistic men compared to narcissistic woman, the first being more men are narcissists than a woman. Male and female narcissists have a prevalent pattern of extreme exaggerations and self-importance, need for adoration, and of course lack of empathy. They both overindulge statements and truths about their abilities and achievements, often being arrogant and ostentatious while undervaluing the accomplishment of others.

Males will use their good looks and charismatic behavior to obtain goals, females use it to gain superiority. Female narcissists become so obsessed with their appearance they will endure several plastic surgeries. Males will use their charisma to entice a significant other whereas a female narcissist uses her body to allure a person into a relationship. Female narcissists love to spend money; they will continually spend even if they do not have the means to support the purchases.

In contrast, the male narcissist loves to make money it can be from their job or a bonus to outright thievery or stealing from others. In a narcissistic relationship if the male is the abuser and believes they are not getting the attention they deserve they will seek it from an outside source and have no problems with cheating on their significant other.

A woman will not usually go outside the relationship instead her abuse will be to emasculate the male in her life. A narcissist will raise a narcissistic child or at the least a child with many emotional issues. In the parent to child narcissist relationship, the parent or the abuser will choose one child to focus all their efforts on, leaving the other children feeling inadequate and useless. Male narcissists view on children is they generally take up too much time because the wife's attention is fixed on the baby when the husband thinks he is important and has all the attention. Female narcissists view their child as an extension of themselves all the way into adulthood and achievements made by that child are a result of their superior mothering.

In their battle at the workplace, male narcissists will see other males or anybody who holds a higher position than they as competition do and female narcissists will battle everyone they perceive as a threat for superiority. Patrimonial followers in corporations happen when employees become personally loyal to their superiors in such a way, they are always seeking approval and are completely submissive to the point they will not act on their own without permission from their employer.

This is what happens when a narcissist is in control or at the head of any company. When a narcissist is in a leadership position, they will first delegate work, then will micromanage to the point of interfering entirely. In this case, if something goes wrong the narcissist cannot be at fault because it was not their project, they had handed it off supposedly. There is an elevated level of stress and anxiety with people who work with or must report to a narcissist causing a higher rate of absenteeism and a large staff turnover rate.

Narcissism cannot succeed in the workplace without codependents. Being in charge may work well for the narcissist but in the end, will not prevail for the company. Narcissism on a job can result in bad decisions that turn costly, will always have negative long-term outcomes and as it spreads throughout it will eclipse the organization by turning it into a totalitarian place to work.

Corporate narcissism occurs when a person with NPD diagnosed or not becomes a member of senior management or CEO of an establishment and gathers a mix of codependents around themselves to support their narcissistic behavior. This will always lead to the deterioration of the entire corporation. In the corporate narcissistic relationship, the abuser will always talk about company loyalty and success but make decisions for the better interest of themselves than the company.

In time this creates a hazardous work environment for the non-narcissist or person who is not codependent since they will not follow along with the narcissist, they will make work unbearable for that person so they will quit on their own actions or give up and leave the position. If they are high enough in a company, they will just appoint their codependents to surround themselves by people who follow their decisions.

The problem in the work environment is the codependents to not recognize their behavior as contributing and meaningful therefore they do not see themselves as the problem. Codependents have been conditioned to follow their bosses' actions and have no responsibility of their own making it even more possible for the narcissist to remain in real power at the company.

Also, in the narcissistic workplace where codependents are being used is that leaders and followers have similar traits, making it all the easier for them to get along and fill each other's unhealthy needs. They both act the same when it comes to avoiding feelings and trying to control future endeavors. Concealing their thoughts and sending mixed messages are both traits of the narcissist and the codependent in a workplace or relationship.

However, the non-narcissists in these relationships are committed to being impartial and pleasant to others and being no confrontational; this only strengthens the narcissists' beliefs in their dominance while establishing their position in the workplace. A narcissistic workplace leads to an emotionally hazardous lifestyle for all employees. The abuser will name call, sexually harass, and act out in aggression towards an employee to help control them.

Having a narcissistic relationship in any form is a type of emotional abuse and along with this abuse comes a substantial list of problems the body will incur physically not just mentally. Narcissistic abuse is one of the cruelest forms of abuse and will cause damaging physiological effects to body and brain. According to recent studies, long-term narcissistic abuse can lead to actual physical brain damage.

Consistent abuse in the narcissist relationship will cause victims to experience a shrinking of the hippocampus while enduring the enlargement or swelling of the amygdala, which leads to disturbing effects. The hippocampus is essential in learning and developing memories whilst the amygdala is where negative sentiments like humiliation, guilt, anxiety, and envy are located.

The hippocampus comes from a Greek word-meaning seahorse because that part of the brain is concealed inside each temporal lobe and shaped exactly like seahorses. One of the most crucial functions inside the hippocampus is short-term memories; information is first kept in short-term memory before being reformed to permanent memory. Cortisol which is a hormone caused by stressed is directly causing the hippocampus to decrease in size. So, the more stressed a person is the smaller their hippocampus is found to be.

The amygdala is popular as the reptilian brain because it handles our primeval operates for desire, terror, and hatred. The amygdala also controls heart rate and breathing. When activated the amygdala is also where our flight or fight response system is located, which is a state of awareness the narcissist will use to keep on constant alert. This will eventually cause the victim to be in constant state anxiety or dread with amygdala responding to any sign of abuse.

If the victim leaves the narcissist relationship, they will suffer from post-traumatic stress disorder or PTSD symptoms, amplified phobias, and panic or anxiety attacks because of the increased amygdala has become too used to living in fear. The victim will often use coping mechanisms such as projection, compartmentalization, and of course denial. Projection lets the victim think the narcissist can be caring and considerate, while compartmentalization can be used to ignore the abuse just as denial is.

The hippocampus is possibly the most crucial piece of the brain when it comes to function and knowledge. A healthy hippocampus helps create new neural pathways because we use it to comprehend, read, and learn. Unfortunately, the hippocampus is damaged every time the body releases the hormone cortisol because cortisol attacks neurons in the hippocampus causing it to shrink. The amygdala is the stimulated by cortisol which causes or neural thoughts to rise our mental acuity to fears and stress.

Among all the emotional distress and brain damage, a victim in the narcissistic relationship is open to many physical ailments. Visual brain damage caused by a toxic relationship is scary stuff and while you can now actually see the physical damage abuse can do on the brain, it is causing the victim to become physically ill. There is also a correlation between autoimmune diseases and the stress internalization the victim undergoes while in a narcissistic relationship.

Adrenal Fatigue, which is not an officially recognized disease, is when your adrenal glands are overworked. Adrenalin is also referred to as epinephrine. The adrenal glands located on top of each kidney secrete hormones such as adrenalin and cortisol and are controlled by the pituitary gland.

Adrenalin is released to help our body respond to dangerous or emergent situations. Your body reacts more swiftly by increasing blood flow to all your muscles and heart, your heart will beat quicker, and your body will use sugar as fuel.

The victim always being in fear of what will happen or what they did wrong will begin to overuse their adrenal glands being in a constant state fright and over the months or years of abuse will cause problems with how your body is supposed to naturally react to emergencies but energy level in general as well.

You are always tired and cannot seem to get yourself going, but once near normal levels of adrenalin do start to secrete you will only be able to get a minimal amount of work done before the narcissist seeks you out to do more of his bidding. This feeling goes on day after day fueling the toxic characteristics of a narcissistic relationship.

Panic attacks or anxiety sound like they are emotional issues but can be a physical trait of being mentally abused. The victim is always in fear of what the abuser may feel or do in reaction to something they did cause the victim to be constantly hyper-aware of every situation they are in. In narcissistic abuse you are always waiting for the proverbial shoe to drop, you know that whatever you may do will never be good enough and you will never satisfy the narcissist.

Never knowing how the one person you revolve your world around can be quite immobilizing. Everything you do you question and ask yourself what will happen when if I do this and what will my abuser say, think, feel, or do. Always worrying about your abuser and never caring for yourself makes you never feel good enough, and since you don't feel good enough your body reacts by panicking to regular situations because your mind no longer knows how it supposed to act. This fearful stage in the narcissistic relationship is also another form of control the abuser uses. By continuously making you so worried, you do not recognize the deterioration the anxiety has done the body, mind, and soul.

One common physical symptom of emotional abuse is hair loss, which comes in three forms, telogen effluvium, trichotillomania, or alopecia areata. Telogen effluvium happens when substantial stress pushes large numbers of hair follicles into a resting stage and inside of a few months starts to fall out when brushing or washing your hair.

Trichotillomania is the urge to pull out hair from your scalp or other parts of your body to help cope with several emotions such as stress, pressure, aloneness, boredom, or even frustration. Alopecia areata is caused by various factors including extreme stress and causes the body's immune system to charge the hair follicles.

Sadly, this is more common among women in the narcissistic relationship than a man is. A rare symptom of trichotillomania is after the victim pulls out their own hair, they are subject to eat it because they are shameful and trying to hide the "crime" however, this will cause them more damage in the long run.

If the hair doesn't pass through naturally and cannot do this in large volumes it will have to be removed surgically, which can be extremely hard to diagnose because it is not the root problem but a symptom of it making the patient less forthcoming. If the hair is not removed it can cause death, but this is an extreme situation referred to as trichobezoar.

Although insomnia does not sound like a physical issue the result of restless nights and lack of sleep will cause your body to deteriorate at a rapid pace. In a narcissistic relationship part of the abuse is to always keep the victim on their toes, second-guessing themselves and worried with how you will react causing you to always be hyper-vigilant. Hyper-vigilance can be extremely hard to come down from because every single sense you have is on high alert and to be able to relax enough to soothe yourself to sleep is a tough task.

Staying asleep would be half the battle if the victim were not plagued with night terrors, grinding their teeth and getting the sweats. Part of insomnia for the non-narcissist in the relationship is having being consistently spied on so even when the victim uses the bathroom they are accused of doing something wrong while in there, from cheating on the narcissist to planning on hurting them, therefore, the victim will lay in bed for hours having to use the bathroom but in fear of what they will be accused of for doing so.

In some cases, the victim will seek out drugs to help them either stay awake or go to sleep. They will find it increasingly hard to do these two basic things and will start to rely on the drugs to the point of addiction. We keep talking about control being such an important weapon for the narcissist, which you will see the emerging pattern of using fear to control.

Your body becomes susceptible to the risk of infection when not taken care of properly.

Skin infections as well as inner body infections start happening or happen more frequently. The victims no longer have the ambition or time to care for themselves, so they put off going to the doctors only causing whatever issue to get worse until they are usually forced to an emergency room.

Autoimmune diseases are very hard to diagnose and pin down but do cause physical limitations and abnormalities for a person. Studies show any stress or prolonged trauma can lead to an autoimmune disease, which does make sense because the autoimmune disease is the body basically attacking its own systems.

Internalizing such negative emotions is giving your body only enough fuel for it to scream for help by making unhealthy attempts at getting attention. Some psychologists believe that the autoimmune disorder was present in the victim before the narcissistic relationship and the extreme discord of the relationship is what activated the disease to affect the victim physically.

Victims having functional and organic autoimmune disease all come from emotional, physical, or sexual abuse as a child. Victims diagnosed with rheumatoid arthritis cite a stressful childhood history of emotional neglect and abuse along with stressful adult histories as well. Adult joint swelling is related to a growth in depression and trouble handling personal conflict. High-stress levels are associated with a rise in androgen-stimulated estradiol and neurohormonal prolactin activity.

Both hormones have been identified in the progression of rheumatoid arthritis and can be linked to the degree the disease can flare up to because it is reactive to stress. In the narcissistic relationship, the victims' control is being taken from them and if they have rheumatoid arthritis during flares or when in pain the sensation to give up is prominent by the victim because they have already lost control of their minds they essentially think they have no control over their body.

Systemic Lupus Erythematosus (SLE) is another autoimmune disease now being linked to victims who have had traumatic and stressful lives. Doctors do not know if SLE is caused by genetics, if it is environmental, hormonal, or caused by drugs taken illegally or by prescription. This autoimmune disease is seen in more women than men, and with people who have a history of emotional deprivation from childhood.

It causes pain or swelling in the joints, fatigue, chest pains, hair loss, and kidney problems to name only a few symptoms. SLE has similar emotional traits to rheumatoid arthritis in the sense that when the victim is feeling hopeless about their disease, they are quick to give up and have the inability to cope with the current effects and stress of the toxic narcissistic relationship.

The neurodegenerative disorder, which the immune system attacks the myelin sheath or the protective protein coating found around nerve fibers causes' inflammation, which further damages the myelin sheath, nerve cells, and the cells that produce myelin is called Multiple Sclerosis (MS). Fatigue, numbness, muscle spasms, problems walking, pain, and bladder or bowel issues are a few of the symptoms of MS.

Victims in a narcissistic relationship who have also been diagnosed with MS share a childhood background of insecurities, unhealthy defense mechanisms such as detraction and denial, and a hard time resolving inner or outside conflicts because of the poor coping skills learned as a child of an emotionally or physically abusive relationship.

Chronic stress from the narcissistic relationship is found to play a role in a victim diagnosed with fibromyalgia. Fibromyalgia has many symptoms such as cramps, stiffness, pain, and fatigue with no apparent structural abnormality in the tissue. It is characterized by having widespread musculoskeletal pain along with memory, mood and sleep issues. Researchers do not know exactly what causes this disease but do believe infections, genetics, trauma, and stress are prime indicators in many victims.

Irritable Bowel Syndrome (IBS) also called spastic colon or spastic colitis affects the large intestine and includes indications of cramping, abdominal pain, bloating, gas, diarrhea or constipation, and in rare cases can cause intestinal damage. Victims with IBS and who are in a narcissistic relationship report they have been verbally and emotionally abused as children, they often cite physical and sexual abuse in childhood relationships.

These victims are more likely to present severe depression and general anxiety in their day-to-day lives; however, this can be hard to distinguish from the same feelings you are going through being a current victim of a narcissistic relationship. It is also found victims who endured chronic threats throughout their lives are less likely to respond positively to any type of treatment warranted for this disease.

All these autoimmune diseases also go hand and hand with one another; meaning most victims who presented with one of these autoimmune disorders were more than likely to have two or more of them combined. These diseases are hard to diagnose because there is no one test that scientifically says you have one of these diseases. It is extremely hard to differentiate between symptoms of the disease and symptoms of abuse also making it hard to diagnose or respond effectively to treatment.

One of the main components for a narcissist in a relationship is an addiction. The victim is under a spell of their abuser which helps them not only gain control of them but to make them codependent on the abuser to the point where the victim becomes obsessed or addicted to the toxic pattern of behavior. The victim of the narcissistic relationship becomes so accustomed to the crazy emotions of their abuser they start to expect and rely on the reaction; in turn, making them addicted to the relationship.

Addiction can take on the form of the abuser in this toxic emotional relationship too. A narcissist becomes obsessed with trying to attain perfection and has influential power over people in their lives to the point where they create their own toxic environment of repetition to live in. They rely on or become addicted to how people perceive them so much to the point where they alter their reality and accept it as a true authenticity of their lives, which is exactly what someone with addiction will repeat of again in a cycle. In the workplace or their relationship, the narcissist is addicted to the feeling of greatness and supreme power and will do anything to maintain it, which is common addict behavior.

Addiction to drugs or alcohol can also take root in the victim of a narcissistic relationship. While being victimized in the relationship you are constantly being told how to act or feel that you do not know the appropriate reaction to anything anymore. Not surprisingly, the victims will find ways to numb themselves it be with alcohol or drugs. Also being in a constant state of fear from your abuser making you be hyper-alert to everything you are maxed out on your emotions.

In a narcissistic relationship part of the control is telling you when you eat, sleep, or when you can leave the house for social or job obligations. These constant directions leave the victims hollow and void of emotions. Without a variety of emotions, you forget how to wake up, or how to go sleep and basic motions a person does on a daily basis. Without raw feelings anymore you can depend on an assortment of medications; uppers to get you going when you need to be alert and focused to using downers to be able to calm down enough to rest or sleep.

Without realizing it, the victim is now dependent on something else and they will believe they cannot do things without chemical assistance. Having an addicted partner in the relationship the narcissist can now use this against you whether it be to berate or belittle because of your addiction or to use the physical drugs against you by hiding them or possibly being the person who provides them for you. Having control over the victim's drugs is now a new way for the narcissist to have more control over their minds and the toxicity of the relationship.

For some victims in a narcissistic relationship will suffer a nervous breakdown. A nervous breakdown has no clinical definition but is a term used to describe a period of mental stress where the body and mind shut down completely and runs on autopilot.

A nervous breakdown comes in many forms and presents itself as severe depression, thoughts of suicide, anxiety, self-harm, high blood pressure, hallucinations, insomnia or sleeping all the time, paranoia and flashbacks. The breakdown occurs from buildup processes such as getting out of bed and going to work or taking care of your children that become impossible and unable to manage.

The exact features of the breakdown vary in degree for every person, it can depend on their history or their current relationship but there will be no significant reason that will be able to be pinpointed to show exactly when the victim started to lose it because it is such a large weight they are used to always carrying. There is no telling what causes these people to unravel but the ability to participate in a social or functional manner along with diminished self-care will only be the beginning of a long journey for the victim of any personality or emotional disorder abuse.

The nervous breakdown does not usually happen within the narcissistic relationship but when it ends. The reason is that the victim is so fixated on their partner and pleasing them, they simply do not have the time nor would they be allowed to have a nervous breakdown, therefore only showing presence in the victim after the relationship has ended. It can happen at any time after the breakup from days to even years to manifest a full out nervous breakdown, but the professional handling the victim should take this extreme show of emotions very seriously.

Unable to have the opportunity to process their past feelings victims of the narcissistic relationship do not seek treatment outright but are brought in for fear of a nervous breakdown or for what presents as a different symptom such as general depression or anxiety.

Victims of narcissistic abuse or in a narcissistic relationship are starting to be labeled as Narcissistic Victim Syndrome or NVS in the psychiatry world and is a relatively new term. NVS victims appear to be nervous and ridden with anxiety with low self-esteem. These victims present with obsessive-compulsive behavior, PTSD, phobias, panic attacks, severe angst, and all-around depression. There is no specific cocktail tailored to NVS, it is a huge mix of emotions along with the suppression of feelings as well.

Dissociation is a coping mechanism employed by the victim for their entire life, because as previously stated current victims are most usually previous victims, for example, being abused as a child and then seeking out an abusive relationship whether it be conscious or a subconscious decision it is the destructive disorder the victim depends on.

By dissociating, the victim can pretend they are not being victimized while saving themselves the trauma of living through the abuse. To dissociate the victim will be going through some type of trauma and project themselves from it as if they were watching it happen to someone else. This strategy used by the victim from a young age can often make the victims rely too heavily on dissociation it because of an automatic response like going numb. By going numb the victim does not have to feel anything either it is physical or emotional abuse.

Somatization is like dissociation because instead of the mind taking a break from reality and stepping out of their body, somatization is when emotion is bothering the victim and not knowing how to react to this feeling, they explain by saying and having cramps or a headache.

In response to anxiety, the victim of a narcissistic relationship will explain it away to a stomachache or cramps.

Victims come out of the narcissistic relationship as over-responsible and willing to take on more than they can handle by always saying yes or agreeing to help someone else out instead of themselves.

By doing this the victim is also able to put off their own needs again and not have to address them if they are busy doing things for other people. One more mentionable trait of narcissistic victim syndrome is the willingness to which the victim will go to, to defend their abuser.

Often the victim identifies and wants to protect their abuser, which is similarly found in Stockholm Syndrome. Stockholm syndrome involves the emotional bonding of the victims to their captors. The victims of a narcissistic relationship learn to align themselves with their abuser because they are unable to see themselves without their abuser. The abuser has made them rely on them so much they really cannot see another life without them.

# CHAPTER 8
# ARE NARCISSISTS VICTIMS?

One of the reasons it is difficult to deal with a narcissist is that you take offense in how they act and what they do to you. It is natural to feel that way. It is especially hurtful if you are dealing with a friend or family member. If your parent is a narcissist who submits you to a toxic relationship, then try to examine yourself. Do you find yourself going over to the dark side by displaying narcissistic tendencies, as well? If this is the case, then your parent – or in some cases, your friend or partner – must have had something done to them for them to have become who they are now.

Here is the tricky part of using the word "victim" to describe a narcissistic person, especially someone who is prone to submitting people to emotional abuse or psychological abuse: he or she more likely likes to play the victim in the first place.

There is a difference, however, between playing the victim and being actual victims. Sadly, a narcissist can do both or be both.

## Playing the Victim

It is hard to confront a narcissist. He will more likely twist the story and make you out as the perpetrator. A child of a narcissistic parent who wants to break away may be labeled as "someone who never cared, anyway". The romantic partner of a narcissist may be verbally abused as a "person who just stays when things are fine." It is hard to be right when around a narcissist. A narcissist is always right, and he is sure about it. He may be paranoid enough to imagine that everyone else has abused his kindness in some way.

## Being a Victim

However, we do have to face the truth. Narcissists are victims, as well.

First, they are victims of circumstance. Who really wanted to be born into this world to be resented and talked about behind his back? Nobody. The terrible behavior of a narcissist can spawn enemies. Yet, he cannot help but feel and act a certain way. He has been trying to find value for himself and yet he does not hesitate to devalue others.

Second, they may be victims of their upbringing. When a child behaves badly, the first people that others will blame are the parents. The circumstances may be completely different from what is perceived, but people cannot help but wonder if a little caring could have prevented the birth of a personality disorder.

Third, they may be victims of genetics. Some people may be prone to taking on the characteristics of NPD.

Fourth, NPD is usually mistaken for a problem with personality and behavior, instead of being a personality disorder. Therefore, people would rather stay away instead of helping the NPD sufferer get treatment or therapy.

It may be difficult to view a loud, arrogant bully as a victim. However, a narcissistic person is usually a hidden type of victim. You cannot imagine him as one, but he will have to continue to struggle with himself.

Characteristics of a Victim Present in a Narcissist

1. Narcissists are sad people.

While narcissists can be loud, it does not mean that they are happy. They are merely covering up a part of them that is suffering. Because they are miserable, they want other people to be miserable, too.

2. Narcissists have low self-esteem.

They do not have a core personality. When you ask about a narcissistic person, he may be described as loud, charming, and talented. Beyond that, you will not be sure as to who they really are. A part of them is aware of this. This makes them unhappy about their core self. They are never content with who they are, no matter how beautiful, smart, or wealthy they are.

3. Narcissists lie a lot and other people are aware.

The sad thing about a narcissist's compulsive lying is that he or she is more likely not aware that he or she is lying. The lies that come out feel like the truth to them and they will more likely believe these lies. Unfortunately, they are not aware that other people can clearly see that they were lying. The awkwardness may only be felt on the side of the listeners.

4. Narcissists cannot live up to their own standards.

Narcissists are perfectionists. They expect other people to be perfect and get very disappointed when they see a glimmer of imperfection. They are like that to themselves, as well. They work very hard just to achieve perfection, even if they have to keep on scrubbing the same floor area in their home. On the surface, however, they just pretend as if they believe in their own perfection. Deep inside, they feel afraid that other people will see through their charade.

# CHAPTER 9
# ESCAPING A NARCISSISTIC RELATIONSHIP

Knowing about narcissism can feel empowering to those who have suffered in a narcissistic abusive relationship.

Is the narcissist to blame? If it's not the narcissist's fault because the cards were just handed to them, should the partner leave? The answer is yes and that a narcissist will always be a snake. The traits a narcissist possess are toxic. Even if they realize it or not, the narcissist will end up hurting those around them.

Most pieces of advice on narcissistic relationships will tell the victim to make a clean break. The problem with this advice is that it's not very practical for some. The victim could have children or financial ties that could make breaking away difficult. A lot of victims cannot just leave town. It might be hard for the victim to see their abuser at stores, work, or other public places.

A narcissist is vindictive, especially a toxic narcissist. They do not want to let go of their victims until they are ready to do so. The narcissist will try many manipulative tactics to win their victim back. If that does not work, then the narcissist will attempt to destroy them.

A victim should never tell their narcissistic partner that they are leaving. If the narcissist knows the victims' plans, then they will do everything in their power to stop them. One technique that the narcissist uses is hoovering. Hoovering is when the narcissist tries to suck their victims back like a vacuum. The victim's partner might apologize for everything that they did, but the apology is not sincere. They may promise to change their behavior in the future.

For a while, the narcissist may revert to their love bombing stage. They try to make the victim forget about past abuse by giving them a taste of how they were before. This stage will not last for long. The narcissist will go back to past behaviors. Any change a narcissist make is temporary.

The narcissist will play on emotions and feelings that the victims still have for them. The narcissist will try to play the victim. They will admit that they have a problem, and they need their partners to help fix it. The narcissist is just using this to manipulate the victim. They rarely recognize that they have a problem. The narcissists will threaten their partner with self-harm if they try to leave.

If hoovering doesn't work, the narcissist will turn to the bait. Baiting is when a person with NPD uses emotional reactions to try and manipulate another person. They will bring out all their victim's insecurities. They will point out flaws in their partner's relationships. The narcissist may point out that they are the only ones who would put up with all their partner's horrible traits. If the victim is afraid of abandonment, the narcissist may act as if they do not care that they are leaving.

The next step is for the narcissist to start throwing out accusations, with little to no truth in them. The victim does drugs, sleeps around, or is just plain crazy. They will tell others these accusations to destroy any social support the victim might have.

If everything else does not work, then the narcissist might result in threats of physical violence. The National Council of Abuse has stated that it takes a partner seven tries to escape an abusive relationship. The victim alerting the abusive partner before they leave will only make the breakup harder.

The first thing that a victim needs to do when planning to leave is to make sure they are financially stable. The National Collation Against Domestic Violence reports that around 85 percent of women return to abusive relationships because of their financial situation. The best action a person could take to avoid this is to get a separate bank account. To keep the abuser from finding out about the bank account, the victim will need a separate P.O box and email. It is also a good idea to make all security questions something that their abusive partner could not easily guess. Some victims wait until their income tax comes in or they get a raise at work to leave.

Sometimes, a victim is completely dependent on the abuser for their finances. The abuser might sabotage the victims' attempts to get a job or gain independents. There are several side jobs that a person could do in their free time available on the internet. Most of these jobs pay through PayPal, which may be easier to hide from a partner than a new bank account. If there is no way that a victim can get financial assistance, and they need to leave, another option would be to seek out a shelter or victim advocacy office. These places can help victims receive financial support.

The victim's credit score is also important. It is important for the victim to note what bills they owe, or what debts they have. This way, it won't come as a surprise later. A financially dependent person might believe a debt paid, like a student loan, only to discover they still owe them money. There are many applications that a person could download on their phone to check their score and who they may owe.

The victim needs to find all their important documents or at least copies of the papers. The documents you need include I.D., social security card, passport, birth certificates, and insurance papers. These documents are important because they help identify who you are. They become even more important if you are living in a country you're not originally from.

If the victim plans on taking the car, make sure that the car is in the victim's name, so the abuser cannot report it stolen. If the abuser has life insurance on their partner, then there is nothing that the partner can do. The partner can change the life insurance they own to exclude their abuser.

If the victim has children, the person leaving needs to contact an attorney or shelter advocate right away. It is important to tell people, so the abuser cannot report the children kidnapped when you leave with them. Tell schools, daycares, and other organizations what is going on. Keeping everyone informed can prevent the abuser from coming by and picking up the children.

Find support away from the narcissist's social circle. By the time their partner is ready to leave, the narcissist has already infiltrated the victim's social circle. The narcissist has won over friends and family. They discarded those they could not win over. The victim should start trying to repair some of their broken relationships if possible; they might feel shame for letting the relationships go the direction that it did. The victim might fear rejection. It might be difficult, for example, to go back to the parents whom they might have spurred.

If the victim feels that they have nowhere to run, a victim advocacy organization could be a good starting point. If a victim does not know where to find such, they can turn to the police or a doctor. Finding a good therapist is also recommended. A family member or friend will not understand everything about the abuse the victim has suffered, but a therapist will help them cope with emotional trauma.

It is also important for a person who is leaving an abusive relationship to get their story out first. Getting the story out is extra important if the victim will have to deal with these people on a daily basis, such as in social gatherings and at work. Being proactive and getting the story out first will stop or at least negate some of the damage that a narcissist might have spread.

The victim should disconnect from all their abuser's devices. Does the device have their email or social media accounts? They also need to check for auto-fill options that may give out their address, phone, and credit card numbers.

When leaving, it might be better for the victim to get a burner phone, and refrain from giving the number to their abuser. The victim should not give their number to anyone who they think will give that information away. If the victim needs to keep their phone number for some reason, then factory reset it. The abuser may attach a tracking app or other tracking software to the phone without their partner noticing.

When planning to leave, it's important for the victim to find a place to stay, which the abuser does not know about. The victim might be tempted to stay at a friend's or a family member's house. While it is crucial to establish these bonds for social support reasons, they don't make the best place to stay. If the victim has a friend that the narcissist does not know about, then that may be the best place to go. The victim would be safer going to an abuse shelter at first, however.

A narcissist may stalk their ex-partners for years after they have left. The narcissist will frequent places that they think the victim might visit. They may visit the victim's friends and family. The victim might also see them in public places, such as their place of work, church, or school. It is important for others to know what is going on. The victim should make it known that they have separated from their abuser and that the abuser might be dangerous.

Contact with the abuser may be unavoidable. In the case contact happens, it's important for the victim to stand their ground. The victim should remind themselves of the reason that they left their partner. They should also not be afraid to get help if needed. It's okay for your child's teacher, your boss, or the police to get involved if the victim feels threatened.

Social media is a good place for a narcissist to stalk their victims. The abuser may make up new accounts and emails to message and email threats to their victims. The narcissist might also talk others in their harem into enacting this type of abuse. If possible, this is the perfect time for the victim to take a break from social media for a while. If breaking from social media is not possible, the victim should make new accounts. The victim should block anyone they do not recognize.

A narcissist will start a smear campaign against the partner that has left them. They will spread their lies through social media and in-person to anyone who will listen. They will act as if they are the victim in this instance. The narcissist is the one who was left behind, and they do not know the reason for it. That is why it is important for the victim to get their story out first.

Another way a narcissist will retaliate is quickly entering a new relationship. One reason that they do this is to get an emotional reaction from their victim. Narcissists love the dynamics of a love triangle. They also do this to appear that they have moved on—the narcissist has already moved to a new person while the victim suffers. To the narcissist, this makes it appear as if there was something wrong with the victim. The victim must have been the problem in the relationship since they have yet to find a new partner. One way a victim can stay out of the emotional drama of the love triangle is to minimize contact with the narcissist.

When children are involved in a narcissistic breakup, they often become pawns in a battleground. The victim can expect a long, drawn-out battle as the narcissist puts up a fight for custody. It doesn't matter how the narcissist views the child; the child is now just a trophy.

After leaving the relationship, the victim should choose a lawyer who is aware of the situation. The lawyer should have some understanding of the narcissistic personality disorder; the lawyer may have dealt with cases of divorce with a narcissist parent before. It is okay to look around until the victim finds a lawyer they are comfortable with.

In court, the narcissist will try to get an emotional reaction from the victim so that they can claim that the person is unstable. The victim should not let the narcissist get to them, so they should try to be calm when they are in public places.

Document everything. It is easy to manipulate text and emails. For that reason, it is important for the victim to save any written correspondence that they receive. If the narcissist has been physically violent, the victim should take pictures of any bruises.

The victim should have a plan and stick to it when it comes to divorce. The victim should know what they want to keep. They should have already decided if they want to co-parent or if they want to get full custody. The narcissist will fight for everything and count every little win as a victory.

The victim should have set boundaries and know their rights. The victims do not have to let the narcissist see the children whenever they want. There should be special days scheduled when the other parent can visit.

Co-parenting will not work with a narcissistic partner. Instead, the victim needs to adapt to the parallel parenting mindset. In parallel parenting, the parents have limited direct contact. The parent gets to do whatever they want with the kid during their time without asking the other parent's consent. If the child, for example, wants to take karate and the practices coincide with the other parent's schedule with the child, they do not have to ask their ex.

The victim should not interfere with the narcissist's parenting of the child. The narcissist might try to use the child to draw the victim back in. They also might try to perform an emotional blow by turning the child against them. If the victim doesn't pay the narcissist's parenting any mind, they can't have it as a tool against you. The parent can give the child a phone to call in case of emergencies.

It's better to pick a place where you can have little contact with each other to drop the child off. It could be at school. One parent drops the kid at school, and the other picks them up. In the summer, you might want to pick a public place as a pickup and drop off zone.

Listen to the child's concerns. The divorce is an emotional time for the child, and they might not understand everything that is going on. The victim should answer any questions the child has as truthfully as they can. The victim shouldn't say anything bad about their ex-partner in front of their child. The other parent may be using them as an emotional chip, and the victim wants to avoid doing the same. Instead, their role in the relationship should be an empathetic ear.

There could be many reasons that the victim of narcissistic abuse does not want to leave. They may want to stick it out for their children, or they may have financial reasons or religious reasons that make leaving unfavorable. The first thing that a victim needs to know is that there is always a way out. Staying in an abusive relationship could be harmful to the body and mind of anyone involved. It is especially important to leave if the victim is suffering from toxic narcissistic abuse.

# CHAPTER 10
# CO-PARENTING WITH A NARCISSIST

You have already learned by now that getting into a relationship with a narcissist is quite easy, despite their abusive behaviors. Then, as a way to keep you involved with them, a little sprinkle of affection here and there can trap you. It's especially easy for someone who is empathetic to stay stuck in the relationship because of their need to help, fix, and justify abusive behaviors. A healthy relationship means that you are not blaming each other, do not pit children against the other parent, and are respectful of each other's privacy and boundaries – all of which the narcissist does not follow, due to their personality disorder. They will lash out at any sign of criticism, threaten you if they know what your weaknesses are, and make you scared to leave them through blackmail. A healthy co-parent relationship is one which sets a structural routine for their children, works together for visits, and supports each other despite the compatibility differences. A narcissist can work their abuse in different ways, depending on the situation.

If a narcissist has the child in their care, they may fill your child's head with lies about you, making you look like the bad guy. This is called projecting their own thoughts, feelings, and behaviors onto you in the child's eyes, so that if the child ever had a choice to come live with you, they wouldn't make that decision. They may manipulate and exploit the child, as their goal is to have the child see them as a better parent to live with and will deceive you at all costs. For example, if it was your day to take your son or daughter, they may tell you that your child is sick and doesn't want to go anywhere. Meanwhile, the child is completely fine and believes you are just unavailable to take them that day. This is a dirty trick where the narcissist fears that their child will have a better time with you or that you will fill their heads with lies about them, so they become the middleman to stop it. If, however, you have your child in your care, the narcissist may make random visits demanding to see them. They may show up at your children's school and tell the teacher that they are picking them up to make you alarmed when you find out your child isn't there. The narcissist may threaten that if you don't give your children to them for primary care, they will make your life complicated and cause a scene in court as a way to blackmail you.

Among this very cruel and disappointing deceit and abusive games, the narcissist's intentions for co-parenting is only to bring you down as your relationship with them hasn't worked out. They are jealous, angry, and prideful, because they are no longer getting the attention from you that you once gave to them. You both are no longer happy from what was most likely a messy breakup and now, the narcissist wants full control. It's good to take a mental note of the fact that when a narcissist shares a child with you, their intent to have the child in their care is not to benefit the child. It is to benefit themselves, as they are no longer getting the admiration they feel they deserve and they want it from your child. Also, it's to punish or get back at you for ending the relationship, even if they were the ones who ended it. With a narcissist you can never win – or can you?

It can be hard to battle the narcissist but against everything no matter what happens in the process, you must keep your focus on your child. Consider your son and daughter above all else and really identify what is in their best interest. If you give into the narcissist's mind games and try to lash out against them, it will fuel their rage and make things worse not just for you, but for your child. For any child, it is hard to acknowledge that their parents had split up – essentially, it's learning how to grow up in a "broken" family. They may feel pressure to have to choose between you or their other parent. Children are incapable of handling such emotional upheaval between their parents, and might rebel or pick sides just to keep the peace.

So, how do you co-parent with a narcissist? The main thing is to keep your composure in every situation. Do not feed into their threats or backlashes. Take their insults with a grain of salt and never lie to your children or speak badly to them about your ex. As 'no contact' may not be able to happen, keep contact only about your children. Make your boundaries clear – if they are going to talk to you about anything else, you will bring the conversation back to the child. Also, make your point clear that if they use your child to bring up a conversation with you about anything else, you will walk away, hang up the phone, or do what you need to do to keep your composure. There are two things you can do to successfully co-parent with a narcissist in a moment of frustration.

Document all conversations while trying to keep a minimal amount of interaction. Download a parenting app where everything is organized and "businesslike" and have all conversations go through this app. This allows both of you to keep the focus on your child, as well as have a shared record of all communication, dates, visitation, etc. If this is unavailable or the narcissist does not want to cooperate in this way, create a planner or journal where you can keep your own notes. By doing this, you can have information and recorded data in case things escalate to having to go to court to fight for your children. All conversations must be professional, straight forward, and if at all it starts to lead to an argument, you have the power to end it. If you don't trust yourself to stay under control, have someone you trust with you to be the mediator and defuse a situation or calm you down, if need be.

Create an organized parenting plan. The moment you officially call your partnership over, make sure that you set up a parenting plan. It's best to have a lawyer or a mediator present to help with this process. A narcissist will rarely abuse you when someone else is around – unless they are malignant. Be sure the parenting plan is very specific, as a narcissist will look for any loopholes to trap you and gaslight you about what was agreed upon. Mark down which days (not weekends) each parent will have their child, who will have primary care, and what should happen on holidays. Explain how transportation will be handled, where and who to communicate if an emergency happens, etc. If you have an organized parenting plan, it will help minimize conversation between you and the narcissist, as you both will know the plan.

"What if I lose control?" Many co-parents have this fear when ending their relationship with a narcissist. We are all human, and it's the narcissist's goal to get a rise out of you so they can use it against you in any way they can. Staying in control is a must, so here are some ideas on how to maintain your composure.

- You are in charge of you – Accept what cannot be changed and move on. During the relationship, your control and sense of self-identity may have been taken from you; however, realize that you control your own actions. You have always had this ability and you always will. It doesn't matter what they do, say, react to, or think, because it is not you or the way you believe things to be. With that being said, let go of what the narcissistic parent does with your child as you will have your own rules and structure. The more you engage with everything they are doing wrong for your child, the more you feed into the narcissist's desire to spite you. For example, even if you put your child to bed at eight in the evening, they may choose to put them to bed at ten or let them stay awake all night. Put aside your beliefs of what they should do and do your best to maintain a healthy environment for your kids.

- Be a good role model – All the things you wish your child to obtain and hold as a healthy, independent individual, you should model. Be empathetic, kind, compassionate, understanding, supportive, forgiving, etc. Whichever emotions or behaviors your child will not learn from the narcissistic parent, make them prominent in your time with your little ones. Give them guidance, structure, discipline, and protection in your attempts to have them grow up into decent human beings. Show your child that it is okay to love yourself while at the same time feeling compassion and love for someone else. Teach them what it means to have empathy for someone, while being assertive is also their right.

- Have a community backing you – All difficult things are easier said than done. The struggle is that the narcissist will try everything from manipulating you into feeling guilty for being a parent, convincing you that they are the better parent, or even trying to win you back to get you on their side again. Every narcissistic co-parenting situation is different. As a narcissist is only out for themselves, they are not hurt by the breakup – they just want to belittle you, drag you down, and have you question all your parenting or personal abilities to handle this situation. They will not care how it affects your child, just knowing that you are suffering makes them feel united and at peace with themselves. The more you show sadness, weakness, or feed into this behavior, the more you are letting them regain their power over you. By having a strong and supportive community behind you, you can get the guidance and positive feedback or criticism that you need to always do your best. This community of people can include your close, trusted friends, family members, and therapists.

The most important thing when co-parenting with a narcissist is to let go of what they say and do and focus on yourself and your child. Basically, act as if you don't have them in you or your child's lives. Maybe it's easier to convince yourself that your children are going to their grandparents for visits. Do not fake your reality, but take on only the stress that shows up in your personal life – not the stress the narcissist tries to make you suffer with.

How to Give the Best Guidance to Your Child

You have learned that they will continue to do things to spite you, manipulate you or your children, and always have their own best interests at heart – not your child's. By limiting contact, setting parental guidelines, providing structure for yourself, modeling healthy communication, and ignoring the narcissist's attempts to abuse you, you can focus more on your child. In this co-parenting situation, your child's development is of crucial importance.

The first thing you must do for your child is to foster healthy qualities which includes:

1. Encourage individuality

Children are influenced by everything and everyone in their world. A narcissist will make them believe that they have to please everyone or "bow down" to their peers in order to feel loved or appreciated. The child of a narcissist is not an individual, but a reflection of them. You, being the non-narcissistic parent, can counteract these habits by helping your child realize that they are their own person. As all children like to follow their parent's lead, make sure to model positive mannerisms to help them figure out the difference between impolite behavior and kindness. Seek opportunities for your child to grow independently such as:

- Providing creative activities
- Asking them which sports or summer camp they would like to join
- Journaling their thoughts and feelings
- Letting them choose their own clothes and toys

## 2. Encourage self-esteem

Self-esteem is built through unconditional love and acknowledgement. Build positive reinforcement through the milestones your child accomplishes in their lives. Give them praise when it's needed, not when they do something to gain your affection. Narcissists have a high, self-absorbed image and so their love will only ever be conditional as long as your child serves them and their needs. More ways to counteract this are:

- Tell your child that they are smart or good (when they are good) to remind them that they have good traits.
- Praise them for things like going potty on their own, winning third place at the fair, or displaying good behavior with their friends.
- Be careful with what you say to them, e.g. – "you are so awesome in my eyes" rather than "you are the most awesome person in the whole wide world."

## 3. Help build self-confidence

Narcissists deny their children self-confidence when they praise them only for their worth to the narcissist. Simply put, they tell their children that they are only worthy and accepted IF they behave this way or think that way. Your child is always taking in new information and building skills so, to boost their self-confidence, reward them by saying things like "wow, you are really good at that, show me again." Or "some things take practice, why don't we try again?" In doing this, you allow your child to figure out what their strengths and weaknesses are, which encourages independence and teaches them to develop confidence in the things they can do while letting go of perfecting what they can't. Try this:

- Sign your child up for a sports team
- Encourage them to try new things
- Explain that being fearful is their body's way of reacting to change and that change is a good thing
  4. Allow mistakes to be opportunities

A narcissistic parent will make sure that their child strives to be the best and only rewards them when they are the best. This promotes perfectionism and results in temper tantrums when your child can't impress. Teach your child:

- Mistakes will happen, but are needed to grow into happy individuals.
- Make a mistake on purpose in front of your child and don't make it a big deal. E.g. – paint together and "accidentally" color out of the lines. Say oops and laugh about it.
- Challenge them to things they don't enjoy doing or are not good at doing, then applaud their efforts and say "good job for trying."
- Do not exaggerate their accomplishments, as focusing too much on this can put pressure on them which encourages perfectionist behavior.

## 5. Create positive influences and environments for your child

Creating a stable environment for your child – one where they will feel safe, secure, and confident – will keep their minds at ease during the switch between parents. As hard as this is on you to co-parent with your ex, it is even harder on your children to adapt to such change. This can also help your child make positive connections and learn from others – not just you.

It's best to remember that you are not perfect – you are only human and you, as a parent, will make mistakes. These mistakes may be that you lash out in anger in front of your child (not towards them), call your ex down by accident when talking to friends, or break down under all the pressure. In fact, these mistakes are needed so that your child can see that you are not perfect, either. They will see that it's okay to make mistakes, as long as we can try to fix them or move forward from them. In all your best efforts as the non-narcissistic parent to develop positive traits into your child, you may not be able to stop the narcissistic traits that may already be developed into them.

So, the second step is to counteract the narcissistic traits in your child. You can do this by:

## 1. Teaching your child empathy

However, it doesn't become a problem unless there is no remorse or feelings behind their actions. You can teach them empathy by: • Always remind them that other people have feelings, too.

- When reading or watching TV, ask your child how they think the person feels.
- When your child does something good or bad to someone else, ask them how they would feel if it had been done to them. This will help them realize the other person's feelings.

2. Explaining the importance of friends and family

Narcissists are usually lonely and sheltered. They rarely have friends come over and they rarely let their child have play dates. That is because narcissists become envious of their children's relationships when they don't have any. For a narcissist, friends and outsiders are people to use, as they are not going to stick around in the long run. Children can pick up on these patterns and use their friends in the same way through manipulation or exploitation.

To counteract this:

- Inspire your child to make healthy bonding relationships.
- Role model healthy interaction.
- Host get-together and invite friends for your child while modeling laughter and fun times.
- Demonstrate loyalty, sharing, and effective communication skills.

## 3. Disciplining and explaining manipulation tactics used by your child

Every child will push limits and boundaries as a way to see what they can and cannot get away with. This is where positive reinforcement and discipline comes in. Simply catch their malicious acts, pull them aside, and explain at eye level how unhealthy this type of communication is. Explain to them a better way to handle the situation and ignore or overlook negative tantrums. When you feed into the positive, you develop positive attitudes. When you give attention to the anger and negativity, it allows them to continue because even through throwing hissy fits, they are still getting a reaction out of you.

- If your child tries to manipulate their friend by saying, "if you don't do xxx, I won't xxx," catch their behavior and tell them that holding something over someone else's head is inappropriate and will not be tolerated. Let them know that they cannot control someone else, but they can do their own thing if their friend isn't playing nicely.
- Role model to them that the kinder you are, the more beneficial rewards you will get.
- Explain to them that through effective communication and being polite, people will more likely want to help you rather than if they fear you.
- Every time they do something positive on their own terms, later, pull them aside and tell them

how proud you are of them for handling the situation the way they did.

## 4. Talking with a professional

Parenting doesn't come with a handbook. You may feel as though you aren't doing anything right, as you will most likely make your own mistakes. Despite your best efforts, your child may continue to bully, manipulate, exploit, and develop narcissistic traits. You may want to speak with a counselor to get more advice or seek guidance from a child development worker on how to fix these patterns.

Even through everything, you will not know what "world" you are stepping into unless you have been there, are going through it, or have overcome it. The best thing to do is to keep a healthy mindset, look out for the best interests of your child, and not give into your narcissistic partner's insults. As it can be quite difficult for a child to live in this type of shared environment, don't worry so much about who they are going to be – put more focus on the fact that you can only do your part as a parent. If your child comes home unbathed, temperamental, or needy, fix what you can, give them attention, and continue your structure. Remind your child that at your house, there are certain boundaries and rules to follow and the behavior they have with their other parent is different. Over time, they will start to differentiate between the two households and know what they can get away with where.

# CHAPTER 11
# RECOVERING FROM A RELATIONSHIP WITH A NARCISSIST

Narcissistic relationships are the most dangerous to go through, and also one of the most difficult to escape from. Recovery may take years, based on the abuse that was forced on you during the relationship. You have already learned what can and might happen through the official breakup, but recovery can be just as hard – if not more difficult than suffering through the actual breakup and its aftermath. Once we begin to understand why it's so challenging to get over a narcissist, we can define each term and work through it individually.

## 1. Normal things were a big deal

As the narcissist took over our lives, they took over our minds. So what was normal became abnormal due to their conditioning and their reasoning behind their abusive ways. We were screamed at for having friends of the opposite gender. We were blamed for telling the truth. We were punished for being honest. We were insulted for being vulnerable. Everything the narcissist put you through changed your way of thinking and, eventually, the way you perceived the world.

## 2. They controlled every aspect of our lives

Did you feel trapped? Like you were walking on eggshells? Did you feel as if your voice and opinion didn't matter? Were your perception and beliefs changed by the countless times that you tried but weren't good enough? This is because the narcissist gained complete control over you, your thoughts, your beliefs, and your personality. They made you question everything, to the point where you felt completely crazy. For example, the narcissist might have tried to find any reason to accuse you of something you have not done, then lash out and threaten you over it. Now, you are going over everything and making sure there is nothing to be found, which only makes you seem guiltier and more suspicious. In a narcissist's eyes, you are always wrong and there will always be a problem.

## 3. We justified their behavior

In the beginning of the relationship, you might have had firm boundaries and beliefs. You had perhaps set strict values and knew exactly what you would put up with and what was not acceptable. Through your relationship, they pushed your limits, invaded your boundaries, and disrespected your space. As a result of these actions, you may have lashed out, acted different than normal, and unleashed your inner beast in retaliation. This was ultimately determined to be your fault, because they can do no wrong. You must forgive yourself for this, as you were in survival mode and your defense mechanisms came out. Part of your recovery is about understanding who you were, who you turned into, then escaping the nightmare to become who you want to be.

## 4. Our realities were distorted

Through abuse tactics such as gaslighting, manipulation, and exploitation, the narcissist used against you things you said, saw, read, or what someone else said, saw, or read. But defending yourself led to thinking up ways that you could get back at them, and maybe even trying to do it; however, it only showed that you had something to hide. Their stories always seemed to change when you asked them about themselves, which would lead to an even bigger argument. Ever get out of the relationship and think, 'I know nothing about them?' Your reality was distorted, because you always had to tell them every detail about your life, how you were raised, and what brings you to the decisions you make now.

5. We never knew who they were

Leaving the relationship, you may wonder if they ever loved you. Did they ever care? What was their purpose in ruining your life? How was any of it fair? What did you do to deserve this? Why do they hate you so much? Why did they say they love you if they didn't show it? The list of questions goes on and on. The truth is, you will never know the answers to these, because the narcissist's behavior was all over the place and didn't make a whole lot of sense. One day, they were charming, sweet, innocent, and real with you, while the next, they were completely vindictive and evil. How were you to know what was real and what wasn't, with the constant whiplash in emotions?

6. Betrayal became part of our worlds

A narcissist is really good at gaining our trust so that we will tell them things in confidence, then later exploit what we told them as a way to use it against us. They may have lied, cheated, played games, or egged you on in an attempt to get an action out of you so that when you did, they could immediately turn around and play the victim card. This is called the trauma bond, where they push and pull, gain your respect, seduce you to blind you, then tug on your heart strings and point out your weaknesses. After looking back on everything, now you feel betrayed, lost, hurt, and worst of all, empty.

## 7. More than the relationship was lost

Like most relationships, you give yourself to someone expecting the same in return. When you break up, they seem to take that part of you with them, but you are relieved or almost grateful for it because you have grown. However, in a narcissistic relationship and breakup, you didn't willingly give yourself to them – they took it from you through their abusive nature and you had no choice but to be vulnerable and try your hardest just to keep the peace. When the relationship ended, they didn't just break up with you, they broke small parts of you everywhere. Look back to what you had and who you were before ever meeting them. Now look at who you are and what you have now. Everything that you were and had is gone. For most people, it is very difficult to accept this reality and move on from this type of emotional and mental abuse.

Outsiders or onlookers may have judged you, and you may have lost some friends along the way because of this relationship. No one truly understands a narcissist's "love" unless they have been in your shoes. You were blinded by seduction, given false hope along the way, and believed that they could be and do better. A way to rise above and recover from the relationship is to gain back the support of others and start taking care of yourself.

## How to Avoid Being Sucked Back In

A narcissist will try to 'hoover' their way back into your life by coming up with creative ways to get ahold of you or know what you are doing. In a way, you could call it a stalker-type way of trying to gain information on you as a way to figure out if you still think of them. Here are some hoovers they will use, and how to counteract them: The Fake Emergency Hoover

The narcissist will often fake a sickness or injury as a way to get you to come to them or visit them in the hospital. They may go as far as actually hurting themselves to win you over. They may use a friend in their attempts as a proxy if you have cut all contact. Their sole intention behind their friend doing their dirty work is: · That you might not recognize or realize that the person is their friend, and you will feel more comfortable taking the bait if it's not directly from the narcissist.

· As the information is not coming from the narcissist themselves, it is easier to believe an outsider.

· The empath will do more for someone who hasn't hurt them if the outsider seems to be in desperate need.

The best way to challenge or counteract this type of hoover method is to see it for what it is. If one of your friends or family members talks about the narcissist all the time, they need some strict boundary rules. Kindly tell the people you know that you would not like to engage in any conversations that have to do with the narcissist – even if they are in the hospital or in need.

The Reverse Hoover

This hoover speaks for itself. The narcissist lets it be known that they want nothing to do with you or your life. They say that they have moved on and that they are surely through with you for good. However, the trick is that the narcissist says this to your friends, family, and people who they know you are talking to. In a way, this is so they don't have to give you closure and that you will come running back to them demanding closure and asking questions. The narcissist knows that with any human being, it is natural to want what you don't have and do what you can't do. So they play on this by letting "your people" know what they think of you – basically challenging you indirectly. When you run to them, they can deny that any of these rumors were said, thus welcoming you into their arms to have you supply their need for attention once more.

To counteract this, avoid acting on impulse or emotion, as the narcissist literally has no empathy. They want what they want and if you feed into the rumors and go asking questions, they will suck you back in with their charm and persuasion. When you hear what has been said, convince yourself that what was said is really true and you don't need closure as you are going to take this opportunity to grow and finally heal.

The Psychic Connection

This will work on people who are especially spiritual. Maybe you have told the narcissist about your beliefs in astrology, telepathy, emotional bonds and connections, hidden communication with animals, etc. If you have, they will use this piece of information to their advantage. The narcissist will reach out to you through a letter or a "sign" that they set up and know only you would be able to notice. From this sign, it may lead you to think of them – maybe you made a spiritual bond when you were together. Now, every time you see this sign, it will trigger you to go be with them. The narcissist will also reach out to you through voicemail or through someone else, stating a dramatic effect on the message that this is strictly 'business' and you must see their mystical awakening immediately. Some examples are: · Claiming they saw you in a dream

· Went to see a clairvoyant who spoke about the two of you

· Their intuition says that you are in trouble and only they know how to help you

· Your name was written in their alphabet soup

The curious or compelling nature of this spiritual side of you wants to go and check it out. The narcissist can be quite convincing, however, it is only a hoover. Recognize it for what it is and do not participate.

## The Silent Hoover

The silent hoover is the narcissist's way to give you your voice. They pretend to allow you closure, but still don't give it to you. You can say what you want, do what you want, lash out however you want, and they don't move a muscle or say a word in response. Similar to the reverse hoover technique, the narcissist will reach out to the people around you and spread preposterous rumors or lies so that you will come to them and speak your peace. An example of this is that the narcissist will post something on their social feed indiscreetly to get your attention, and only you or your friends would know it's about you. Then, as you find it insulting, you will have the need to reach out and explain what really happened.

If you feel the need to explain yourself, only explain to the people that matter the most to you. Do not reach out to the narcissist, do not try to persuade them to remove the post, If you do, it will only cause conflict, and they will have sucked you back in by using the trauma bond to get inside your head again.

## A Bonus Hoover

I don't know what to call this hoover technique, but this actually happened to me. I was cleaning for a friend at their house and I got a text from my ex. He acted as if he was a woman, feeding into my jealousy. First, he asked what I was doing, and I didn't respond. Then, after a couple hours of silence, I got curious and texted back, "what do you want?" He then replied with, "sorry, you have the wrong number." I acted out in anger and demanded to know what he wanted. Then, he sent me a picture of a woman (probably something he got off the internet). Through my rage, I said confidently in a smart way, "Oh, honey, don't feel special, he has had lots of girls in his bed." He then responded with, "He calls me magick." Feeling insecure, I then texted back and said, "He called me that, too, so I hope that makes you feel better about yourself." I then put my phone away and congratulated myself for not participating in his wicked game. The next message I got, however, pushed me over the edge. It read, "I love the color of your hair extensions, they look really good on me." I am quite territorial, so I didn't text back as I had forgotten my extensions were left at his house and drove there as fast as I could. When I got there, I opened his door with the key I still had and found that everything was as I had left it. He wasn't home, and all my stuff was neatly packed by the front door. What happened next was cruel and debilitating but, long story short, he came in not seconds later and needless to say, sucked me back in.

What did I learn from this experience? That he was a full-blown narcissist and I would never return. I am now free of the narcissist and I have never felt more empowered than I do today after my experience with my ex.

## Learning How to Heal

Every step involved in the healing process takes time, energy, patience, and commitment. It may seem foreign, at first, to gain some clarity and be one with yourself again, but with practice, it will seem natural again. Healing does not start until you have officially left the narcissist and know within your heart and soul that you are not going to go back. Now, the very first step before anything else you must do is to create a safe place. Make sure that your no-contact is in place, and if you share custody or have a child with this person, cut ties emotionally. Every interaction you have with them (for those of you with children only), act as if you are so bored or uninterested that there is no emotion coming from you. Instead of saying, "oh, wow" and getting excited for it, show no interest whatsoever in front of them. Act as if it's not a big deal and you couldn't care less. When you look at your child to send them off, express happiness and gratitude by saying "you are going to have so much fun with mommy / daddy, be good and use your manners. I love you and will see you when you are home." When you show no interest or emotion towards them, they will assume you have moved on and that they hold no power over you anymore. Once you go back inside or when you are alone, then you can release your emotions, whether that be screaming, kicking a wall, or venting to a friend.

You may not feel as though you have control, or maybe that they do still have power over you. The main thing is to not act like it, because as long as you are working on yourself and trying to heal from their abuse, this will come in time. The goal here is that you take back the control and power they took from you and now give it to yourself through love, affection, and treating yourself in the way you deserve to be treated. A positive way to look at this beginning stage in your healing is that you would never be able to have this opportunity if they didn't come into your life. Every person is in our lives for a reason, whether they were intended to stay or not. The thing about heartbreak and rough times is that we will always have stress and there will always be problems. It's all about how we manage them, how we learn and where we grow from them that counts. Also, there is no right or wrong way to heal, as everyone is their own individual and heals in their own ways based on their perspective and strengths. Always have goals, take risks, meet healthy relationships, start a new hobby, go to the gym, read positive affirmations every day. Do what you weren't "allowed" to do when you were with them, which will help you gain a new perspective on freedom and will feel really good.

Here are four steps to healing:

Step One: Exercise

Exercise heals different parts of our bodies at different rates – especially our brains. It releases the same hormones you get during intimacy and helps you stay calm in a stressful situation. At first, you can start by doing beginner's guided yoga or light stretches as you inhale and exhale slowly through the exercise. The more exercise you do, gradually you will have more confidence in yourself to get moving more and more. The first day might be that you stretch in bed, the fourth day that you do yoga on the floor. The next few days, you may even have the energy or motivation to dance or jog. Once this motivation hits, make sure that you continue to exercise, as there are so many health benefits that combat stress revolving around exercise.

Step Two: Walk and vent

It doesn't matter whether it is a nice, sunny day or if it's a cold, wintery and snowy, a walk in nature or even just around the block will help clear your mind from all burdens. Vent to the nature around you – get out what you need to say. Don't feel crazy if you need to talk out loud, but initially, the goal is to get rid of your pain and baggage so that you can move on and heal. On your walks, focus on your internal energy, ask questions to the "Gods" and every day after, look for signs that point you in the right direction. When you cry in nature, allow the wind and "Mother Nature" to carry your weakness away. Allow your voice to carry compassion within yourself. When you feel at ease, more at peace, and one with yourself, only then can you be aware of what you would like for your own future.

Step Three: Write

Sometimes, the best release is when you can write it out, read it back, and gain a different perspective. The thing about journaling is that you can feel confident that no one is going to read your words unless you allow them to. You can write without editing and say whatever comes to mind without feeling bad for it. Journaling can connect you with your thoughts, emotions, behaviors, perspectives, and beliefs. It is so healing in the fact that you are taking back your own voice and can scream it all on paper until you are confident enough to say these things out loud. Often, people will hold their thoughts in and bottle up their emotions as a way to ignore them because they are too painful. By writing them out, you are releasing the negative energy you hold in your heart and welcoming positive energy flow from your daily exercise and self love strategies.

Once you are able to release all your dark emotions and hurt feelings, you can finally start writing about the more positive things you have done. Try starting a gratitude journal or a positive self-reflection journal. Do this every day before bed or before you start your day so that you can grow in all your future endeavors.

Step Four: Newness

Newness is about trying new things, adapting to changes, and getting out of your comfort zone as a risk-taker. When you engage in these new adventures, you may find a new awakening or enlightenment. You will feel inspired from the growth that you didn't know you had before. This will help you stay forgiving of yourself and thankful for the narcissist's experience in the role they played to get you here. Personal growth is about how you looked at things, and then how you choose to look at things after the fact.

Have you ever created a bucket list before? If not, create one now and if you have, find it and add some more things. Where did you always want to travel? How many kids do you want to have? What kind of people do you want to meet? Do you have a preferred culture or language you want to learn more about? Pick something from your list and start planning how you can achieve these goals, then slowly work towards them once a month, one a week, or even every day. When you finally do complete something from your list, you will have come so far from who you are now that the newness of it all will help you in making your future decisions just for you. The goal is to make yourself happy in all that you try to do.

# CHAPTER 12
# THE STEPS TO HEALING

There are five things you need to release from yourself when you have just undergone the terrible abuse and consequences from a narcissistic relationship. First, you need to accept the pain and give yourself time and patience to grieve the relationship. Just as every emotion and relationship needs attention from you to be able to let it go internally, a narcissist does, too – but only to yourself, not them. If you hold on to pain and grief, you are holding onto hate and negativity. Healing takes time, and you need to come to an acceptance of your self-worth and self-respect to regain your true character or identity, as the narcissist has robbed this from you. Next, you need to release the illusion or the lies you told yourself about this person. A narcissist does not deserve justification or empathy for their patterns and habits, and you shall no longer be controlled by their power over you. From this, we can move onto the forgiveness of the betrayal that you may have deep within yourself, but also from what the narcissist has made you feel. Betrayal is a dark feeling that, if held onto, everything you see and everyone you meet, you will question and potentially be setting yourself up for another abusive relationship. Releasing the injustice that was done to you can bring a new sense of enlightenment as you learn to let go of the pain that the narcissist caused. This next part may be the most difficult step, but the connection may still remain even after feeling the sadness of letting go of betrayal, and defining who they really were and are. If the connection still lies with them, they will always be able to win you back, or you may find yourself in another narcissistic relationship. Once all of these steps are completed, you can finally feel liberated from the experience and at peace with yourself, as this is your ultimate goal after any form of bad relationship.

## Releasing Pain and Grieving the Relationship

It's normal to grieve a relationship, as it allows you time and space to let go of the painful times and open yourself up to better experiences in your future. By grieving the loss of your relationship and all that your ex took, you will no longer be triggered by the trauma they put you through because crying or feeling sad over it is actually the first step to letting them go. Grief comes with a number of sub–emotions like sadness, confusion, anger, guilt, shame, disorientation, etc. Here are a few things you can do to help with the grieving process of your breakup to promote healing.

1. Let it all sink in

Confusion comes from the questions of trying to figure out what went wrong and why. At first, you may be feeling shocked or frustrated because the thought of them not being around anymore has not set in fully. What are you going to do now? Because of how dramatic and debilitating the narcissist was, you may have revolved your whole life around someone else. As a result of this, you may not know how to start paying attention to yourself. They didn't just take your heart, they took your whole life and the person you were so confident being before.

You may feel that you can't live without them due to how dependent you become. You may have an overwhelming urge to run to them and beg for forgiveness – even though you did nothing wrong. In this time of the healing stage, you will experience 'abuse amnesia' which is essentially your mind's way of forgetting all the abuse they put you through in an attempt to deal with the shock.

This is the stage of the process where you may want to party, drink, rebel, and lash out like you couldn't do in your relationship. If this is what you need to do, make sure you come back to reality after a few days, as this is not healthy and there are easier and better techniques to get over the pain.

2. Don't fight the way you feel

Let your feelings come – feel them, don't ignore them, then gradually allow them to leave. It's like breathing –

if you were to hold your breath, you would die. Now, imagine holding in your emotions: your sense of feeling and that part of you would slowly die. This would make future emotions difficult, thus leaving you empty and non-empathetic – or worse, someone who lashes out on everyone and everything. If you are sad, be sad, cry, let it out. If you are angry, be mad, scream, let it out. Give yourself permission to grieve the loss of your relationship. It is okay and it is very needed for your healing process.

3. You come first

This is perhaps the most important step. You come first. As much as this may seem selfish to you, know that you cannot please or impress everyone. Also, you cannot help someone if you are not fully capable of helping yourself. Self-care is crucial in this stage, otherwise your grief and sadness can quickly lead to depression. Make sure that if you are skipping meals that you are at least snacking through the day. If you are losing sleep, try to have a nap every day to catch up.

No one can tell for sure how long this grieving process will last, as it is different for everyone. Once you go through the ups and downs of the grief and confusion, each day will come easier as you work through it.

## Release the Narcissistic Illusion

Narcissists are con artists. They get to know you really well early on through the information you share with them, and they are also reading you, as well. They are good people readers, and so when they see you as empathetic or caring and nurturing, you are their target. They figure out what you suffer with, what your "love language" is, and get to know your deepest desires so that they know what type of façade to put on – how they are going to act to have you fall for them. They spin their charm web, cast their love spell, and put a trance on you right in the beginning, all by finding out what type of person you are so they can be the "perfect partner." This is the narcissistic illusion.

The faster you can wrap your head around the fact that the narcissist was never who they pretended to be, or that you were deceived by their little game, the faster you can start to release the pain that comes with their dirty illusion. For example, if you suffer with a type of anxiety disorder, the narcissist would make you feel comfortable and relieved by rubbing your back or helping you through a breathing exercise. They may lie about someone they knew that struggled with anxiety, or tell you that they are well-equipped when it comes to panic attacks as they have this special skill to calm people. All the while, you may be feeling calm and collected from their relaxing aura, but you are actually falling for their trap. One of the main tell-tales of a narcissist is that it is habitual for them to bring up a story or talk about themselves – no matter what.

To release the illusion you have been dealt with is to first forgive yourself for falling in the first place. Do not label yourself with "I am naïve," or "I am pathetic." You may feel ashamed for falling for the charm but ask yourself, would you blame yourself for crying when watching a very convincing movie? No, you wouldn't, so why should you blame yourself and label yourself as anything less because you fell for the "act" of the narcissist. You are human and you are loved. Tell yourself positive affirmations by complimenting yourself or rewarding yourself when you do good. Don't strive for perfection, strive for what you can do and don't feel bad for what you can't. It's not your fault you were blindsided and, through this illusion and con-artist's tricks, you can officially say that you are stronger because of it. Be grateful for your experiences and stay positive for what's to come, as nothing worth accomplishing is easy.

## Release Feelings of Betrayal and Injustice

When you hold onto these feelings of injustice and betrayal, you will want to seek revenge. This anger will slowly build up inside of you until one day, you won't be able to hold it in any longer. Not everything needs to have justice served, as you can be sure that karma will come to these dark souls and take care of it for you. Find a greater power and release this bad energy into the world so that you are no longer holding onto it. As long as you hold onto this energy internally, you will always allow the narcissist to keep hold of you. The goal is to not take whatever the narcissist says and does personally as a way to combat their abuse. When you take it personally, you allow the pain, anguish, and trauma to build up, thus leaving you helpless, sad, and hopeless to ever finding love again.

By holding onto the betrayal and remembering everything that the narcissist did, you are taking away from yourself and your ability to focus on what really matters. What matters right here and right now is that you no longer have to suffer. You can finally be free and feel liberated through the experience as a means to grow, not suffer. As long as you continue to focus on the pain that lingers and wonder what they are doing or not doing, you are feeding them "the narcissistic supply."

1. Stay compassionate

It is just as important to take care of yourself physically as it is to take care of your mental health, as well. By being compassionate and sympathetic with yourself, the feelings of betrayal and anger will stay at a comfortable, manageable level. Make room for compassion and kindness, not anger and hostility.

2. Is it worth it?

Is it worth spending all your time and attention feeling angry and betrayed by what they have done? How do you allow yourself to grow when you are focusing more on them than yourself? Decide that they will no longer have this power over you. You will no longer resent them or give the relationship any more attention than you already have. If you do, then you take away from yourself right now, and right now is crucial to grow not stay stuck.

## 3. Fact and emotions

Ask yourself, what are the facts? And how do these facts relate to me? Why do I feel the way I feel? How long will I allow this to control me? The fact of the matter is that you dated and were wronged by a narcissist. The fact is that they cannot be changed and they do not have the empathy or kind heart that you do to hold on to pain and betrayal. Instead, they are too busy trying to boost their own ego and can never see the wrongness in their actions. Only you can, and holding onto this only stunts your ability to see past it and heal.

## 4. Be patient

There is no rush – it is not a race to overcome these feelings. Every step of the process takes time and you must be patient with yourself, Allow yourself as much time as needed to dive into every emotion revolving the circumstances of your relationship. While also being patient with yourself, do not stop taking care of yourself and searching for positive things to do every day, as this will boost your mood and self-confidence.

Betrayal, anger, resentment, and injustice can swallow you up if you don't learn how to manage these emotions effectively. Everything that has happened was not your fault, nor was it the narcissist's fault. Yes, they abused you and robbed you of your sanity among other things, but they most likely grew up in an environment that was unstructured and unhealthy, which made them who they are today. This is no excuse for their actions, of course, but thinking more in this way will give you the ability to process or make some sort of sense out of it. Betrayal comes from the feeling of not knowing why and having unanswered questions with the shock and surprise of an event. To let this go, just be peaceful and compassionate for yourself – the more time you spend working on positive thoughts, the less time you can concentrate on anger. The brain cannot process two emotions at the same time, so feed it goodness, and you shall have goodness in return.

# CHAPTER 13
# TIPS ON HOW TO HELP
# A NARCISSIST

After your experience with a narcissist and having understood now what made them who they are, you must wonder if there is anything you can do to help them. Are they even treatable?

Infantile damage as the cause of narcissism is hard to cure, even impossible. It is so deep-seated and protected by the false self, not to mention the narcissist refuses to acknowledge their vulnerable self. On the other hand, you may be able to help them unlearn acquired narcissistic behaviors.

The question of whether you can help a narcissist is not what is most important. The real problem is that narcissists usually do not want to change. To do that, they need first to understand that their actions are wrong and cause negative feelings to the people around them.

At the same time, they must want to change and hate the feeling that their actions evoke. They must hate it so much to the point they do not want to feel that way anymore. With that understanding, the narcissist must choose a different action from what they usually do even if it will upset them.

## What Will Motivate a Narcissist to Change?

A narcissist chooses to change his ways for selfish motivations. It is a motivation that does not have anything to do with others. Even when they decide to change, the reason is still always about them, and that is why you cannot really appeal to them.

Words Won't Sway Them

Telling a narcissist that you want them to change their behavior because it hurting you or upsetting you will not work. Swaying him this way will only result in negative reactions.

For instance, telling your feelings to the narcissist means you want him to feel remorse. But it is not something he can feel since he lacks empathy. On the other hand, he knows shame. When shamed, it triggers anger and puts them on the defensive. Keep in mind that the narcissist never cares about your feelings.

Logical Reasoning Doesn't Work

Speaking about a narcissist's feelings, they consider them as real and true. Of course, that is not true and would be unreasonable. But you cannot reason with a narcissist whose mind does not operate the same way as normal people. It means the only way to encourage them to change is it must be on their terms.

Change Happens by Overcoming Behavioral Patterns

Those defenses formed a protective shell called the False Self to shield their true vulnerable self. It is how they gave themselves permission to be the way they are right now. The False Self is an aspect of the narcissist that is going to be really hard to break. Narcissists are children and helping them change means encouraging them to grow up.

## Treatment Options

The biggest help you can get for a narcissist is professional help. It is a mental health condition that will not be easily changed with simple home tips. The narcissist is going to need treatment to break their negative behaviors. It may not be curable, but it is possible to treat it so they can have more meaningful relationships.

Psychotherapy

The leading treatment for a narcissistic personality disorder is psychotherapy. It involves therapy sessions individually, with groups or with the family. The goal is to help the narcissist understand the causes of his behaviors and beliefs. At the same time, therapy helps them learn ways to relate to others effectively.

Narcissists lack empathy, which is essential to understand other people. Can it be learned? According to research, it can. This is great for narcissists as therapy sessions on empathy might help them to be considerate of the experiences and perspectives of others.

With a considerable amount of therapy, pathological narcissists may learn to take responsibility for their choices and actions. It may also aid them in learning how to create realistic goals. It is the fundamental aim of therapy to teach narcissists how to have and maintain good personal relationships.

Medicine

Another option is medicine. Some medications are effective in treating NPD. However, most of these medicines are only used for managing certain conditions accompanying the narcissistic personality disorder such as anxiety and depression. Therefore, it does not directly treat narcissism.

## Treatment Takes Time and Effort

As you know by now, it is a huge problem to help a narcissist to change when they do not even want to, given their inherent nature. Narcissists do not like to appear weak, and to them, receiving treatment is a sign of weakness. If your loved shows signs of NPD, getting them to realize their problem is necessary.

Once they recognize it, you must continue to encourage them to ask for professional help. Treating a narcissist needs time and effort since it is a deep-seated problem. More so, narcissists likely will not agree to be treated if they do not see it as the only solution left.

If you really want to help your narcissist parent, partner, or friend, it is essential that you remain as patient and encouraging as you can. It is a little complicated trying to let them know of the harm their behavior is causing. You need to be careful in how you say it, or it can become a disagreement, which leads to rage.

And as I said before, an angry narcissist is not much of a listener. Don't push him too hard as it may make your efforts to get them to treatment in vain. The best approach to help a narcissist is a residential treatment because it will take long-term therapy sessions for any changes to happen.

When in a residential treatment facility, the narcissist can truly focus on changing his behaviors while in an environment without any distractions. It will be good for them to be in a place without anything that will stress or provocation. At the same time, access to experts' help is easy.

Seeing the problems caused by a narcissistic personality disorder, it may seem hopeless to help them. It can also be fearful as one wrong move might end up with you being sucked into the manipulations of a narcissist. If you want to help your loved one who has an NPD, you need first to learn to be assertive.

You need to have plenty of self-love and confidence in yourself to protect you from the narcissist. Things may not look up at the beginning but don't lose faith. When you are confident in yourself and have complete control over your life, you have the power to help a narcissist.

## How You Can Support a Narcissist's Change

If your desire is to support a narcissist towards change, one thing you need to learn is the use of empathetic confrontation. You can sympathize with them, but it is important not to let yourself be swayed. As I said before, assertiveness and confidence in yourself important.

In the methods mentioned below, you can help the narcissist while also protecting yourself. They are essential practices that can lead to the narcissist to learn the consequences of their actions and begin to change. See that you apply them whenever you have to deal with a person with narcissistic behaviors.

Set Up Clear Boundaries

Always keep in mind to maintain these boundaries as they are a key part of having a successful, functional relationship with a narcissist. From the start, tell the narcissist the behaviors you will not tolerate and the consequences of violating them.

Try to See Things in Their Perspective

As a reminder, don't react to anything a narcissist does. Instead, respond after taking a moment to see things from his perspective. When you see their reasoning or intention, act in a way that will not provoke them either positively or negatively. Make sure to keep a neutral stance with a narcissist.

Use Empathy to Get Them to Empathize

This one is going to be tricky. After all, narcissists lack empathy. Your goal here is to get them to copy you, hoping they will model their behavior on how you show empathy. In this method, you have to provide them with plenty of examples of how to be empathetic. Listen to them and try to understand their feelings, but don't justify it.

Celebrate Small Victories to Keep Them Motivate

Another way of showing a narcissist your support is by being there to celebrate the little achievements he made. Through meaningful consequences, it is possible to let a narcissist know of the need to change their behavior. It will give them a solid motivation, a balanced external and internal reason to want to change.

When you are there to show them that his efforts are appreciated, he can feel more motivated to be less narcissistic. Simple words like "Thank you" when you hear him say "I'm sorry" for any narcissistic behavior is a great way of praising him.

The fact is that therapy is hard for narcissists inherently. They will need positive encouragement to continue on this path. Similarly, it is crucial to limit criticizing their behavior as much as you can. Still, do not let go of your leverage and always make it clear to the narcissist that their actions and words have consequences.

As someone who has been used and abused by a narcissist, it must be hard to try to help him transform for the better. No one will blame you if you choose to stay away and focus on yourself.

# CONCLUSION

Narcissists will target empaths for the sole reason that empaths feed their need for attention and self-righteousness. Normally, empaths are people who are already self-insecure, but show it more dominantly than the narcissist does. These personalities paired together make for a very toxic relationship. Narcissists use abusive techniques and methods such as gaslighting, manipulating, controlling, blackmailing, and exploiting their victim or partner. As much as I would like to say they cannot help it due to their upbringing, everyone has a choice in their actions and with proper communication, the narcissist can choose to do better and act more appropriately. However, because they cannot handle any sort of criticism as they find it abusive and victimizing, they would first need to let go of their own perfectionism before they could change their ways.

If someone has had a child or multiple children with the narcissist, they don't only have to heal and overcome the abuse on themselves, but have to watch out for their children, as well. It's one thing to get involved with a narcissist and another to raise one. In order to break the cycle of narcissism, you need to learn how to counteract the side effects of narcissistic parenting methods.

From ending a relationship, to knowing what happens next, to protecting yourself, to finally knowing how to recover from the aftermath, you can finally start to heal. Healing takes time, and it is the act of releasing the toxic and negative energy from your mind and body to grow into what you have longed to be. The narcissist robbed you of your belief that you can do better and be better.

From this moment on, it is entirely up to you on what you wish to do and exactly how you can do it. Do you finally want peace and freedom? Of course you do – so, from this moment on, use these methods to grow and heal from any trauma you have experienced thus far.

It is the personality disorder that can have adverse effects on both the person with narcissism and those around them. It is the idealization of themselves, the self-love, and admiration for themselves that creates a reflection in which they look into and only see the good in themselves. Yes at times, the traits and characteristics can be positive in terms of achieving success but we know now that it is the way in which they got to the top which has created this feeling within us. This feeling, in part, was bestowed upon us by the narcissist - the feeling of never being good enough, the feeling of being unworthy, that we will never amount to anything in life. We are not seen as people with emotions and feelings which can be hurt; we are seen solely as people who appear to be obstacles, hurdles, and challenges. We are not on their level in any capacity because they refuse - or are rather unwilling - to open up emotionally and see the true extent of their behavior, their actions, and their words.

They bask in the glory of themselves. They want us to recognize their success and to applaud them because of that. They want to be the star of the show, the hero, the victim – any way that they can get our undivided attention and adulation.

They are this way to us because of the pleasure that they feel when they see our faces shift from happy to sad, hurt, and offended. They enjoy the feeling of watching us feel upset because of them. And for this, they are vindictive individuals and they manipulate us, addicted to the supply of emotion in which affects us. And for this, they are narcissists.

However, now we can understand them. We can see the reasons why they are the way that they are and we are now able to formulate our own strategies in which to use to our advantage.

We have been abused by them physically and mentally and now we know why they are the way they are and why they will never change or find it difficult to change. We now know how to deal with them; how to avoid them; and how to cope and heal from their abuse. We have to celebrate ourselves for overcoming our pain and we can appreciate the efforts that we have made to deal with narcissists in our lives.

I hope it has shed some light on this subject and can help you! For the narcissist reading this who is on a journey of trying to change, all the best. I hope you will be able to see the emotion around you in this world and to be a part in it. It is commendable what you are doing, so for the sake of those who love you, keep going.

We are people who are all guided by our own paths and emotions but the underlying fact is that we are all people who get hurt and all people who, at some point, need to heal.

www.ingramcontent.com/pod-product-compliance
Lightning Source LLC
Chambersburg PA
CBHW070711250726
48662CB00001B/359